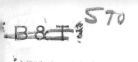

MESSNER'S
INTRODUCTION
TO THE
COMPUTER

MESSNER'S INTRODUCTION TO THE COMPUTER

FRED D'IGNAZIO

Julian Messner ⟨M⟩ New York

For
Dorothy Pierce deGoza
and
Margaret Webster Stevens

Copyright © 1983 by Fred D'Ignazio

All rights reserved including the right of
reproduction in whole or in part in any form.
Published by Julian Messner, a Simon & Schuster
Division of Gulf & Western Corporation.
Simon & Schuster Building,
1230 Avenue of the Americas,
New York, New York 10020.
JULIAN MESSNER and colophon are trademarks of
Simon & Schuster

Manufactured in the United States of America

Design by Irving Perkins Associates

Library of Congress Cataloging in Publication Data
D'Ignazio, Fred.
  Messner's Introduction to the computer.

  Bibliography: p.
  Includes index.
  Summary: Discusses the history and future of computers,
focusing on stories of the pioneers behind computer
developments.
  1. Computers—Juvenile literature. [1. Computers]
I. Title. II. Title: Introduction to the computer.
QA76.23.D5 1983   001.64   82-42881
ISBN 0-671-42267-7

PICTURE CREDITS:

Hewlett-Packard, Pg. 37

Bell Laboratories, Pgs. 28, 79, 80, 81, 85 (bottom), 121

IBM, Pgs. 40, 63, 64, 65, 68, 69, 123

James A. Gupton, Jr., Eddie Cook, and Scott Carter, Pg. 23

Intel Corporation, Pgs. 84, 85 (top)

Trilogy Systems Inc., Pg. 87

Amdahl Corporation, Pg. 88

John Poulton, Henry Fuchs, and the University of North Carolina. Photo by Mike Pique., Pg. 93, 94

Henry Fuchs, Computer Science Department, the University of North Carolina at Chapel Hill, Pg. 95

Lynn Conway and the Xerox Corporation, Pg. 96

Lynn Conway, Xerox Corporation, and Stanford University, Pg. 97

Sperry Univac, Pgs. 107, 109, 142

Bruce Goldstein, Pg. 72

William Eventoff (Perkin-Elmer Corporation) and the British Computer Society, Pg. 102

Institute for Advanced Study, Pg. 111

Shirley Lukoff. Photograph originally appeared in Herman Lukoff's book, *From Dits to Bits: A Personal History of the Electronic Computer*, Robotics Press, 1979. Photo reprinted by permission of the publisher., Pgs. 140,141

Atari Inc., Pg. 44

Antony Miles Ltd. and *Computerworld*, Pg. 114

Charles Freiberg. Reprinted by permission of the editors of *onComputing*. Copyright © 1980, *onComputing*, Byte Publications, McGraw-Hill, Inc., Pg. 145

Scott Adams and Adventure International, Pgs. 47, 48

Claudia Napfel and Charlotte Knadle. Photo originally appeared in the 1979 issue of the *Hobby Computer Handbook*. Photo reprinted with the permission of the editors of *Elementary Electronics*. Pg. 139

Reprinted with permission from the editors of *onComputing*. Copyright © 1980, by *onComputing*, Byte Publications, McGraw-Hill, Inc. Pg. 147

Woodrow Seamone and The Johns Hopkins University Applied Physics Laboratory, Pg. 165

Woodrow Seamone, Wolfger Schneider, and The Johns Hopkins University Applied Physics Laboratory, Pg. 166

Robert N. Gordon, Pg. 149

Alan Kay, Pg. 153

Photograph originally appeared in the February 1981 issue of *BYTE*. Reprinted by permission of the editors of *BYTE* magazine, Copyright © 1981, *BYTE*, Byte Publications, McGraw-Hill, Inc. Pg. 167

Mary Robinson and the Deaf Community Center of Framingham, MA., Pg. 168

Frederick P. Brooks, Jr., and the Computer Science Department, the University of North Carolina at Chapel Hill, Pg. 125

Joe Liles and the North Carolina School for Science and Mathematics, Pg. 170

Larry Press (Small Systems Group) and *SigPC Notes*, Pg. 177

Drew White, Bell Laboratories, and the Computer-Based Education Research Laboratory, the University of Illinois at Urbana-Champaign, Pg 174

From the computer-assisted instruction lesson, "distill," by Stanley Smith. Copyright © 1975 Board of Trustees of the University of Illinois. Reprinted by permission of Control Data Corporation. Pg. 175

Ted Horowitz and *onComputing*. Copyright © 1981 by *onComputing*, Byte Publications, McGraw-Hill, Inc., Pg. 179

Edward Feigenbaum, the Stanford University News and Publications Service, and the Heuristics Programming Project. Pg. 192

Harold Cohen. Photo by Becky Cohen. Pg. 197

Dr. Hans Berliner and the Department of Computer Science, Carnegie-Mellon University, Pg. 198

Jonathan Kaplan. Photo by Flora Kaplan. Pg. 202

Unimation Inc. and Warren Joli Studio, Pg. 206

Unimation Inc. and *Robotics Today*, Pg. 205

Dr. James Albus and the National Bureau of Standards, Pg. 208

David H. Ahl and *Creative Computing*, Pg. 214

Computer design and programming by Dale Ingold. Courtesy of the SAS Institute, Inc. Pg. 216

Molecular coordinates courtesy of D. and J. Richardson, Duke University; super-oxide dismutase enzyme with copper and zinc atoms and ribbon plot by Mike Pique, University of North Carolina, using MOVIE. BYU program

ACKNOWLEDGMENTS

I FEEL LIKE a pioneer myself after all the winding, unmarked trails I had to follow to track down the stories you'll find in this book. On these trails, I met nice people who answered my questions, gave me some pointers, and sent me off to do some more exploring.

I want all these people to know that I am grateful for the contributions they made to this book. My thanks and a tip of the hat go to:

> **Jim Albus** *(National Bureau of Standards, Washington, DC)*
> **Marty Auman** *(National Bureau of Standards, Washington, DC)*
> **Hans Berliner** *(Carnegie-Mellon University, Pittsburgh, PA)*
> **Peter Blake** *(Robotics Today, Dearborn, MI)*
> **Fred Brooks** *(UNC, Chapel Hill, NC)*
> **Esther Carter** *(Sperry Univac, Blue Bell, PA)*
> **Ed Catmull** *(Sprocket Systems, San Anselmo, CA)*
> **Hal Chamberlin** *(Micro Technology Unlimited, Raleigh, NC)*
> **Becky Cohen** *(La Jolla, CA)*
> **Harold Cohen** *(UCSD, La Jolla, CA)*
> **Nancy Connors** *(Mainstream, Washington, DC)*
> **Lynn Conway** *(Xerox PARC, Palo Alto, CA)*
> **Ann Dooley** *(Computerworld, Newton, MA)*
> **Lisa Dreske** *(Intel Corporation, Santa Clara, CA)*
> **Presper Eckert** *(Sperry Univac, Blue Bell, PA)*

Nancy Estle (BYTE, Peterborough, NH)
David Evans (Evans & Sutherland, Salt Lake City, UT)
Bill Eventoff (Perkin-Elmer, Tinton Falls, NJ)
Myles Falvella (Digital Press, Bedford, MA)
Ed Feigenbaum (Stanford University, Stanford, CA)
Henry Fuchs (UNC, Chapel Hill, NC)
Bruce Goldstein (St. Paul, MN)
Bob Gordon (Glen Rock, NJ)
Jim Gupton (Charlotte, NC)
Mark Haas (BYTE, Peterborough, NH)
Phyllis Handsaker (Evans & Sutherland, Salt Lake City, UT)
Tom Holub (Bell Laboratories, Short Hills, NJ)
Lori Holzer (USC, Marina Del Rey, CA)
Marcia Hunt (UNC, Chapel Hill, NC)
Jonathan & Flora Kaplan (New York, NY)
Alan Kay (Atari, Sunnyvale, CA)
Don Knuth (Stanford University, Stanford, CA)
Peter Kuhn (IBM, Armonk, NY)
Shirley Lukoff (Fort Washington, PA)
Karen May (Sperry Univac, Blue Bell, PA)
Lynne Novicky (Unimation Inc., Danbury, CT)
Mike Pique (UNC, Chapel Hill, NC)
Gloria Poetto (IBM, Armonk, NY)
Harry Press (Stanford University, Stanford, CA)
Larry Press (Small Systems Group, Santa Monica, CA)
Mary Robinson Deaf Community Center, Framingham, MA)
Woody Seamone (Applied Physics Lab, JHU, Laurel, MD)
Debbie Sloan (NYIT, Long Island, NY)
Carroll Snead (UNC, Chapel Hill, NC)
Arnold Sorenson (Information International, Culver City, CA)
Pam Sorlie (University of Illinois, Urbana, IL)
Nancy Stern (Hofstra University, Hempstead, NY)

Charles Strauss *(Providence, RI)*
Marcia Sutherland *(Pittsburgh, PA)*
Henry Tropp *(USF, San Francisco, CA)*
Andy van Dam *(Brown University, Providence, RI)*
John Whitney *(Santa Monica, CA)*

I would like to offer a special thanks to my wife, Janet Letts D'Ignazio. Without Janet's support, this book would have never been completed.

CONTENTS

Part VI

A Computer in Every Bedroom

Part VII

People Helpers, Spaceships, and Turtles

Part VIII

Thinking Machines and Robots

Part IX

Creative Computers and Computer Genius

A Word
to the Reader

YOUR IMAGINATION IS a wonderful thing. It is as endless, as boundless, as space and time.

You can express what you imagine in words—by talking or by writing on a page.

Computers are such amazing machines because anything you can imagine, anything you can write down or say, can be fed to a computer. The computer can store it away in one of its tiny, electronic cubbyholes. Or it can combine *your* ideas, facts, and visions with other ideas, facts, and visions. You can be the computer's only teacher—its only source of knowledge or information. Or all human beings can be its teachers.

The computer is an electronic genie, and you are its master. Do you want music? The computer will translate your ideas into musical notes. Do you want pictures? The computer will translate your ideas into tiny blocks of color on a TV screen. As in painting by numbers, the computer combines the little blocks and gradually forms a picture.

The computer knows no boundaries. As long as you have an open, active, inquiring mind, the computer can take you to all kinds of wonderful places.

Part I

FOR JUST 25 CENTS YOU CAN SAVE THE EARTH

1

COMPUTER HEROES AND MONSTERS

THE HERO AWAKENS in an alien, nightmarish world. His whole body vibrates from the musical notes that echo through the blue-walled maze that surrounds him.

He looks to the right. Directly ahead is a narrow pathway. Hovering above it are large white lights, like rows of bulbs in a carnival sideshow. The bulbs are bright, but cast no light on the eerie blue walls.

The hero spins around. There are more white lights, more blue walls.

What was that? A noise, faint at first, grows louder. The hero is frozen with panic. The noise becomes an awful din. The hero whirls fearfully to the right, just in time to see a sky-blue monster—a stubby-legged octopus—round a corner and race hungrily toward him.

The hero must escape. But how? He has no legs.

But he can move. He moves by eating. His round, fuzzy head looks like a king-sized yellow grapefruit, except when he opens his mouth. Then he can swallow things whole. He can eat the glowing white lights. He can even eat the octopus monsters—but only when they have become powerless.

For the hero to disarm the hungry monster closing in on him, he must eat his way through a corridor full of white lights. Then he must gulp down a giant bulb, almost as big as he is.

The blue monster is coming closer. The hero races off through the maze, gobbling lights as fast as he can.

The monster chortles and chuffs hungrily. If it catches the hero, it will sink its teeth into him and pop him like a balloon. His body will shrivel up. After a final squeak, like air escaping from a bicycle tire, he will disappear.

The hero will not let that happen. He gobbles white lights even faster.

He races around a corner of the maze, searching frantically for the magic light that gives him the power to eat monsters. But he has taken the wrong turn. The monster closes in on him. He is caught. A moment later, it is all over. The hero is gone.

Like a bulging vacuum cleaner, the stuffed and happy monster glides away. Within seconds, it is hungry again. It begins stalking a new hero.

There he is, in the same spot where the first hero appeared.

But this new hero is smarter. Almost as soon as he appears, he races down the corridor, madly munching the white lights.

He rounds two corners of the maze. Right behind him are three monsters, yapping musically, closing in for the kill.

The new hero is tricky. At the last second, he darts into a pitch-black tunnel and disappears. The monsters follow him into the tunnel, but they are too late. The tunnel floor grabs at their stubby legs. Their mad dash for the hero slows to a turtle's crawl.

The hero emerges from the opposite end of the maze. He has made a clean getaway. Like a racehorse, he whips around the corner headed for a superlight and the power to munch monsters. He'll gobble the light, then ambush the monsters at the tunnel's mouth.

THE PUPPET MASTER

The heroes and the monsters live in a tiny, flat, maze world on a sixteen inch high screen. Directly above that world is a sheet of clear glass. The glass acts as a window into the creatures' world.

Suspended above the blue-walled maze is a huge face. Blue and white lights from the maze bounce off huge teeth. The face's lips are parted in an enormous grin.

At the bottom of the maze a giant hand grips a red knob. The knob is perched like a meatball atop a huge metal pole buried in a wooden box. The hand jerks the knob up, down, then to the right, then back up again.

Each time the knob moves, so does the yellow "mouth man" hero inside the maze. In fact, the hero is controlled by the knob.

The hand belongs to the face. The hand and face belong to a person. Like a puppet master, the person guides the little hero through the maze, gobbling white lights and blue monsters.

Who is the person? His name is Vann Larimore. As Vann races his tiny hero around, he glances nervously at the upper lefthand corner of the maze. White numbers roll by, like the numbers in a gasoline filling pump. The numbers grow steadily larger. They represent Vann's score. Each time the mouth man eats a light bulb or monster, the numbers swell.

Vann occasionally loses a hero. But a new hero appears to take its place. Vann plays on—thirty minutes, fifty, seventy, eighty.

At ninety minutes, his concentration falters. A pink monster appears out of nowhere and gleefully devours the last hero. The game is over.

Vann looks at his score: an incredible 750,000 points. He has won the city tournament. He is the best Pac-Man player in Winston-Salem, North Carolina. He slumps into a chair, proud but exhausted.

SOLDIERS ON PARADE

Tucked away inside the Pac-Man game, and inside millions of other electronic games, are thin plastic circuit boards. Lined up on the boards, like soldiers on parade, are rows and rows of tiny computer chips. The chips are the electronic "brains" that control the games' action.

When you pop a quarter into a game, creatures, spaceships, even whole worlds spring to life on the game's TV screen. The heroes and monsters that materialize on the screen start their lives as electrical pulses in the memory of a tiny computer chip.

Once there were only a few computers, hidden here and there, in great universities, spread across the world. Compared with today's computers, the old machines were big, heavy, and slow. An old computer was like a dinosaur—a huge, lumbering brontosaurus. Its cables were as thick as jungle snakes. And it had thousands of tubes that looked like hot, glowing pickles. It belched out answers to arithmetic problems at the rate of one per second.

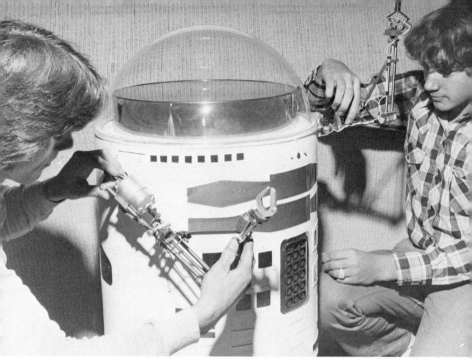

Cornflake-sized computers can fit inside any appliance or machine, even a robot. Here students at the Union County Career Center in North Carolina are building a robot that will eventually have a small but powerful computer brain.

Over the years the python-sized cables shrank to the size of ropes, then strings, then threads, then hairs—until today, the contents of that room-sized computer fit into a tiny pea-sized chip that can whiz through a million addition problems in a single second.

It's a long journey from a scientist's brightly lit laboratory to the blaring rock music and the murky darkness of electronic game arcades. But the beeping, flashing, talking machines in the arcades are all computers. Their complex game rules and tricky moves are stored as blips of electrical energy. Their pictures, sounds, and voices are all controlled by tiny chip "brains."

Electronic computer games are irresistible. For just a quarter, you can save the earth. Or enter a colorful, fast-moving world on the edge of the galaxy. Or journey into the future. You can leave your mom, your dad, and your kid sister or brother behind and blast off on a mission of danger and adventure. You can enter fantasy worlds of attacking insects, leaping frogs, deadly piranhas, and monstrous, girl-snatching gorillas. All for twenty-five cents.

Or you can play at home on video games and home computers. Or you can whip out your pocket-sized Pac-Man or electronic football game and play at the breakfast table. Or just roll up your sleeve and push the GAME button on your watch. The time fades from the screen. In its place appears a mischievous monkey that starts throwing coconuts at you. If you catch the coconuts, you hear music. If you miss, the monkey chitters at you and fires another bunch of coconut bombs.

All these games have computers inside them, remembering rules, flashing game pictures and music, and trying their hardest to challenge and beat you.

A WORLD OF INTELLIGENT MACHINES

Have all computers become wristwatches and games?
Hardly.

Tiny computers are now hidden in hundreds of different everyday machines. They are the secret brains that control the machines and make them cheaper and more reliable. There are computer chips inside radios, calculators, and television sets. They are inside new telephones, typewriters, microwave ovens, dishwashers, and automobiles. They are inside stop lights, guitars, and cash registers.

Experts predict that chips will soon appear inside eyeglasses, tooth fillings, credit cards, furniture, and clothes. Already, people with certain physical disabilities have chips surgically implanted in their bodies.

New chips that give blind people a form of electronic sight are now being tested in laboratories. The chips absorb light, then send a message that bypasses the damaged eyes and goes directly to the brain. The brain records an image similar to the one sent by a sighted person's healthy eyes. For the first time, perhaps since birth, the blind person can "see."

Our world is moving to a new, fast-paced computer heartbeat. Rock music is being produced on computerized instruments, then recorded by computer on records. Computers help human artists produce some of the movies' most dazzling special effects. Athletes train for the Olympics with help from computer "coaches." The athletes use gloves and boots with tiny computers inside, and computer monitors are taped to their bodies.

Deaf people chat over the phone using computer typewriters. Old people confined to bed, inmates in prisons, and people in mental institutions have jobs teaching desktop computers. How do they get their work to their employers? They use the computers to send it over the phone lines like electronic carrier pigeons. Often, the companies they work for are located across the country or across the world.

Elsewhere, computers inside small briefcases accompany country doctors making their rounds. Computers inside robots work alongside factory workers in automobile factories. Football-sized robot pets live in teenagers' closets and emerge for arm-wrestling and chess matches with their young creators.

Other computers work on oil platforms in the middle of the storm-tossed North Atlantic, telling geologists and oceanographers where to drill for oil. Computer-controlled robot mice scamper through mazelike mine shafts and along miles of crisscrossing air and sewage pipelines. Computer-controlled robots dive hundreds of feet into cold water to service undersea mines, factories, drills, and "farms." Computer-controlled robot photographers whisk around the solar system, snapping photos of Saturn's rings and Venus's dirty, sand-and-acid hurricanes.

Tiny computer chips are everywhere—under the sea, over our heads, in our clothes and on our bodies. Many people still see computers as giant calculators, as paper pushers and bill collectors. And they still are. But they are already much, much more.

This book describes the amazing evolution of computers. We will start with the inventors of the fabulous new electronic games. Next, we'll journey back in time and visit the huge, warehouse-sized machines that took a second just to add two numbers.

Later, we will return to the present and look at new supercomputers that operate at incredibly fast speeds. We will discuss computers that teach, computers that help disabled people, and computers that act as the brains of robots. We will look at creative computers—computer artists, musicians, and moviemakers. Last, we will speculate about computers of the future—computers that are alive, and superintelligent computer geniuses.

Throughout our journey, we will look at computers through the eyes of their creators—the brilliant men and women who are inventing wonderful new computers even as you read this book.

2

JOURNEY INTO
AN INVISIBLE
WORLD

COMPUTERS USED TO be gigantic machines the size of your school gym. Scientists had wanted to put computers on spaceships, but they were too big and heavy. So the scientists found ways to shrink them. Finally, an entire computer was able to fit on a square piece of silicon that could hide under a dime. The little computer was called a *chip*.

A chip is so small it could ride on the back of a ladybug. It could hide in your sock, behind your ear, or under the tip of your tongue.

Computer chips are midget masterminds. In a single second, they can do a million addition problems or remember a hundred thousand birthdays.

Computer chips run on electricity. If you looked at a chip under a microscope, you would see what looked like thousands of tiny tunnels crisscrossing like a maze across the face of the chip. Those tunnels carry the electricity that makes the chip work. They dive and swoop through a sliver of silicon as thin as a human

This computer brain is smaller than a telephone push button, yet it contains 45,000 transistors and can perform a million calculations a second. It will be used in talking, singing telephones that can obey spoken commands.

hair. Silicon is an element, like oxygen or gold. There is silicon in sand. Walking on the beach on a bright, sunny day, you can see it sparkle.

DOWN THE RABBIT HOLE

The world inside a computer chip is a fascinating place.

Imagine that you shrink until you are incredibly tiny. You become the size of one of the little tunnels of electricity inside a computer chip.

You are now in a world so small that a flea looks as big as a whale. An ant hill looks bigger than the world's mightiest volcano.

This is the world inside the computer.

In this world, pulses of electricity race like lightning through millions of microscopic tunnels.

You look around. In the distance you see a round tower as tall as a skyscraper and as wide as the Houston Astrodome.

You move closer. It's not a tower. It is a human hair. Watch out!

A red blip of energy whizzes past you.

You are surrounded by whirring objects the size of basketballs. But they are spinning like buzzsaws.

They are all different colors. They whirl so fast, they are almost a blur.

These buzzsaws are particles of light. Deflected by droplets of water, they make a rainbow. Scientists use them like a surgeon's scalpel to dig new tunnels for electricity to follow inside a computer chip.

Scientists are finding ways to make the little tunnels even smaller.

Already they are so small that a scalpel made of light is too big and clumsy. Now scientists have to use even sharper scalpels made of X-rays and electrons.

Some computer chips may soon be so small that scientists will be able to paste dozens of them, like plastic tiles, on the surface of a red blood cell.

Someday we may be able to build computers the size of a few molecules or a few atoms.

And as computers get smaller, they get faster.

THE TWO WORLDS OF COMPUTERS

Computers may be getting smaller and smaller. But we humans are big. Each of our fingers is wide enough to spread across a million tiny computer cells. A whisper from our lips would be like a raging hurricane in the tiny, fragile world of computers.

How can we use anything that delicate or that small?

We can because we have developed machines that carry messages back and forth between our large, human world and the tiny world of computers. When messages are sent inside the computer, they speed up and grow smaller. When the messages return, they slow down and grow larger.

How does this happen? What are these machines?

First, there is an elaborate system of wires inside a computer, each smaller than the last. The smallest wires are almost microscopic. These wires plug into the chip. The next wires are a little larger. The next larger still.

Eventually the wires hook into three machines: a typewriter, a TV screen, and a tape recorder. These three machines allow us to communicate with the tiny computer chips.

We push the buttons on the typewriter to enter information and commands into the computer. We look at the TV to see information the computer prints out. The information might be the computer's answers or new questions. It might be words or a colorful picture.

When you turn off the electric power, everything in the computer chips is erased. Therefore, you need a tape recorder. You use the tape recorder to store the computer's important commands and information when it is shut off. Later, when you turn the computer back on, you can feed everything back in directly from the tape recorder.

THE INFORMATION MACHINES

You've learned about the two worlds of computers. But what makes a computer different from all other machines? Computers are changing so fast, how can they be described?

Close your eyes and try to picture the actors in a vaudeville sideshow. The actors play many roles and wear brightly colored costumes. As soon as they have played a role, they exit from the stage, run to their dressing room, and put on a new costume. In a moment, they are back on the stage playing a new role.

Yet no matter what role they play, no matter what costumes they wear, they are actors with the same set of skills. Underneath the roles and fancy clothes, they don't change.

Computers are like actors. They are changing, shrinking, and playing hundreds of new roles. Yet, underneath, they remain the same.

Each day we hear about new computers that are smaller and faster. We hear about how computer transistors and switches may shrink to the size of a molecule—or even smaller. We hear about computers so fast that, every second, they can erupt in a giant outpouring of facts and figures that would fill a New York City phone book.

We hear about new roles for computers. We hear about computer doctors, robot scientists, and computers that play music. We hear about computer pets, computer watchdogs, and computers that design other computers.

But, just like the actors, on the inside computers remain the same. No matter what they look like, no matter what they do, they are *information machines*.

As information machines they have only three jobs. First, they must receive information. Second, they must digest that information. Third, they must act on the information in some way (like print a number, or play a musical note, or send the results back to their human masters).

That's it. Everything computers do involves one of these three basic tasks.

You can feed computers any kind of information. Then they can manipulate the information in an endless number of ways. Computers don't have to work alone. They can perform their duties by controlling other machines—trucks, spaceships, missiles, mechanical hands, wheels, and robots. A computer can be taught to control any other machine ever invented.

Computers are extremely versatile. When the computer has finished a task (mixing chemicals in a dye plant or figuring out an orbit for the Space Shuttle), its memory can be erased. Then the computer's teacher (a scientist, a doctor, or you) can feed the computer a new list of instructions—a new *program*—to make it do something new. You can do this over and over again. The computer can keep learning as long as you are willing to teach it.

All computers run on electricity. Someday we will have computers that run using rays of light. They will have gigantic memories and be much faster than today's machines.

Most computers, known as *digital computers*, use electricity of a special kind. The memory cells inside the computer are like tiny light switches. They are either on or off. That means they either have a small charge of electricity or they don't.

The little charges of electricity are known as *bits*. Strung together, like beads on a necklace, they can represent numbers, letters, dollar signs, musical notes, or the answers to riddles. The way the bits are arranged is important. If the bits are arranged in different patterns, they mean different things. For example, ON-OFF-ON might represent the number 3. ON-ON-ON might represent the number 7.

3

THE KNIGHT
AND THE CHIP

IMAGINE THAT A villainous knight leaves his crumbling stone castle and walks up to your computer. The evil knight raises his huge, razor-sharp broadsword, then whacks it down, chopping your computer in half. His dirty work done, the knight grins at you and then disappears.

At first you are horrified. Then you get curious. What do the insides of your computer look like?

Inside the computer you see lots of snakelike wires, twisting and turning, skinny and fat. The wires connect the TV picture tube to some green plastic circuit cards about the size and shape of graham crackers. Riding on the cards are neat little rows of computer chips.

In fact, most circuits—transistors and other devices—inside a modern computer have been shrunk to chips the size of cornflakes. These fingernail slivers of silicon may have a million or more parts. Grouped together, the parts perform two jobs: they remember things and they shuffle information.

PENCILS, SCRATCHPADS, AND GENES

There are two types of memory chips—RAM and ROM. The RAM (Random Access Memory) acts like a pencil and a scratchpad. When you feed your computer new instructions, it "writes" them down in its RAM. When you tell the computer to obey your instructions, it remembers where in RAM it wrote them down, then fetches them at high speed. Then it obeys them, one at a time.

If you turn your computer off, your information and commands in RAM instantly disappear. (Unless you have stored them on a tape recorder.) This is not so with another kind of memory called ROM (Read Only Memory). Unlike RAM, ROM is permanent. The information in ROM remains and is still there the next time you turn your computer back on.

But you can't store information in ROM. Information on ROM is canned and prepackaged. ROM is like buying a scratchpad already filled with notes.

ROM chips are also like your genes. Your genes carry information that tells what color your eyes will be, whether you will be short or tall, and how your body will grow and develop. You have no control over the messages inside your genes.

Similarly, you can't change the message in ROM chips. They were loaded into ROM in the computer factory. Then they were burned in or "frozen." The ROM circuits contain valuable information that may tell your computer how to paint a picture, speak in a human voice, perform difficult calculations, or play a challenging game of football or space war.

An arcade game may use dozens of ROM chips. Some of the chips store the game's rules. Others store the game's fabulous pictures. Still others store the game's sound effects—the tunes and the spectacular explosions.

You can't actually see the ROM chips in an arcade game. But one place you can almost see the chips is inside computer game cartridges. A game cartridge is a plastic case the size of your wallet. Inside the case is a little ROM chip.

To hook the chip to your game computer, you just plug the cartridge into a hole on top of the computer or on its side. Once the cartridge is plugged in, the game computer can read the information and game rules stored in the cartridge's memory.

THE GAME BRAIN

There are computers inside all the video and arcade games. But what do they do?

This is where the second part of the computer comes in: the computer brain, or *processor*.

The computer's processor is like a traffic cop or an air traffic controller in your local airport. Information comes zipping into the processor in the form of strings of bits—ON/OFF pulses of electricity. The processor must figure out what each string means, what should be done with it, and where it should go.

The processor also has some basic skills. It can perform arithmetic. It can make decisions. It can take strings of bits, break them apart, switch them around, and then re-combine them into something new. In this way, the processor can make new words, numbers, and information.

In a computer game, the processor must obey orders coming from two sources. First, the game's rules are stored on a tiny ROM memory chip. The processor fetches the rules, then obeys them to play the game.

Second, the buttons and joysticks on the front of the game are wired to the processor. Whenever you press a button or pull on the joystick, you instantly send a command for the processor to obey.

By pushing a button, you might be firing a laser cannon or launching a photon torpedo. By pushing the joystick, you might be moving a soccer player or a purple-and-green spaceship.

GAME PICTURES

How does the processor "draw" a cannon, a torpedo, a soccer player, or a spaceship on the game's TV screen?

There are two types of game picture screens. First, think of a screen that goes in a window in your house. If you look at a window screen up close, you can see little boxes formed from the screen's crisscrossing wires.

A TV screen has boxes, too. You see them when the processor sends a command to light them up or "paint" them some color. Each little box on the screen has a special address, like a wall of mailboxes in a big-city post office. No two addresses are the same.

The processor can paint one box. Or it can paint lots of boxes together—all over the screen and in lots of different colors. In this way, it makes a game display. The display might be a baseball field, an underground maze, or a river swarming with ferocious piranhas.

And the other type of game screen?

Again, think of a window screen. Only this time, when you look at a screen up close, look at where the wires crisscross. Look at the points.

Some game screens are like window screens: they are filled with tiny points instead of boxes. The computer processor draws pictures on the screen by connecting

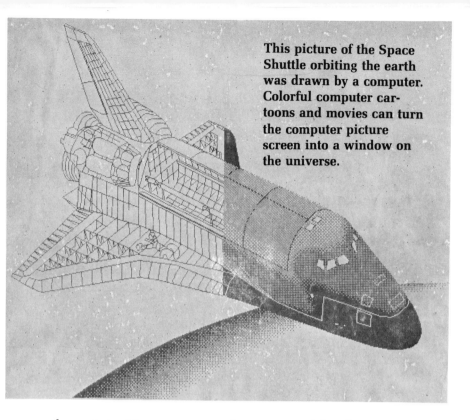

This picture of the Space Shuttle orbiting the earth was drawn by a computer. Colorful computer cartoons and movies can turn the computer picture screen into a window on the universe.

the points. Have you ever drawn something by numbers? Each number has a point and you connect all the points, one after another, to make your picture. The processor makes game pictures the same way. It connects the points and makes tanks, flying saucers, old-fashioned airplanes, football players, and alien invaders.

EXPLOSIONS AND CHEERS

This is how the computer makes game pictures. But how does it make a game's sound effects?

A computer's commands and information start as electric charges stored in its tiny ROM memory. When the time comes to make a bomb explode, a whistle blow, or a crowd cheer, the computer translates the electrical charges into sounds. In the same way, the computer can create voices and music. It translates stored patterns of electricity into waves of sound.

The computer takes a long string of ON/OFF charges and translates them into numbers. These numbers represent a sound wave. A sound wave looks like a big breaker off the California coast. It can be represented by a string of numbers that start small, grow to a peak, or crest, and taper off back to nothing.

The processor sends the numbers representing a sound wave to a special device that creates an electrical wave that mimics the real sound wave. The device shoots this wave to a pair of speakers like the ones attached to your stereo. The charge of electricity causes the speakers to vibrate, just like drums hit with a drumstick. The vibrating speakers create real sound waves that ripple through the air.

The ripples of air emerge from the electronic game and enter your ears. Your ears translate them into sounds—robot voices, songs, firecracker explosions, police sirens, screeching tires, and cheering crowds.

4

THE PEOPLE INSIDE THE MACHINE

THE FIRST COMPUTER was built over a century ago by Charles Babbage, a lone inventor working in a laboratory in his home. Unfortunately, Babbage's computer was never finished.

Almost a hundred years later, the first modern computers emerged, the creations of small groups of men and women working in university laboratories. Each year only a couple of new computers were born. Building computers took a lot of time.

Then, all of a sudden, computers became popular. Factories began turning computers out by the dozens, then by the hundreds. The computers found their way into businesses, universities, military bases, and government offices.

The computers got bigger and more complicated. They cost millions of dollars. One person working in a private lab could no longer invent a new computer. Neither could a small team of scientists or engineers,

Charles Babbage tried to build the world's first computer almost a century and a half ago.

no matter how brilliant they were. Now it took hundreds of people spending huge sums of money and years of their lives.

Then, thanks to a single invention, all that changed. Scientists found a way to squeeze an entire computer brain onto a *chip*—a flat block of silicon smaller than a postage stamp and as thin as a human hair. Chips were small. Chips were cheap. Once again a single person in a basement workshop could build his or her own computer—complete with typewriter and TV screen. Building personal computers became a popular new hobby.

The computer continued to shrink. Today, some companies sell computers for less than $100. The new computers are as powerful as the million-dollar machines of only twenty years ago, yet they sit on top of a table and consume the same amount of electricity as a light bulb. Very few people build their own computers today. You can buy a computer cheaper than you can make it.

But, once again, we are entering an era of "homemade" computers. Scientists have discovered ways to use computers to help build other computers. Students in college are using these computers to design totally new computers. They are inventing superfast, super-powerful computers, all for a few dollars.

In a short while, these tools will be available to high school students and hobbyists. Once again, people working in the classroom, workshop, or study will be designing and building revolutionary new computers. These computers may perform tasks no one today has even dreamed of.

PIONEERS AND FRONTIERS

This book is about computers—where they come from and where they are going. But we are not going to look just at the machines. We will look at computers through the eyes of their creators. There is a story behind almost every part, transistor, and command inside a computer. In each story, there is a computer pioneer—a person who saw computers not as they were but as they could be.

To capture all the great moments in computers or spotlight all the important computer pioneers, a book would have to be as long as an encyclopedia. Here you will find a collection of snapshots—quick sketches of computer pioneers, their dreams, and their machines. You will meet the people who built the first computers. You will also meet many of today's pioneers. These engineers, scientists, and young people are at work, right now, building revolutionary new computers of the future.

Part II

THE GAME
WIZARDS

The Atari Video Computer System.

5

KING PONG

IN 1962 STEVE RUSSELL, a graduate student at MIT, wrote a computer program that ran on MIT's large computer. The program didn't solve physics problems or figure out complicated math formulas. Instead it was a game—an electronic game. Steve called it Spacewar.

During the 1960s, Steve's game floated secretly from computer to computer. People were only supposed to teach computers how to do serious work. Instead they were teaching computers how to play Spacewar.

Early in the 1970s, Nolan Bushnell, a student at the University of Utah, learned about a program similar to Spacewar. He used a copy of the program secretly stored on his university computer. Nolan quickly grew tired of the program. After making several improvements, he was still not satisfied, so he scrapped the program and tried to develop something new.

Nolan figured that the Spacewar-type games had gotten too complicated and abstract for most people to understand. Also, they were not fast-paced enough to challenge people and maintain their interest. Nolan worked on the problem for a while and came up with an electronic paddle-tennis game. He called the game PONG. Next Nolan built a game computer using some tiny new computer chips, and he programmed PONG into the computer. Nolan built the world's first tabletop video game.

By this time Nolan had left the University of Utah and had moved to California. To see if anyone would like playing PONG, Nolan loaded the game into his car and carried it over to Andy Capp's Bar in nearby Sunnyvale. The manager of the bar agreed to let Nolan put the game in the corner.

Twenty-four hours later, Nolan went back to the bar. The manager told him that PONG was broken. Disappointed, Nolan pried open the lid on the machine. A fountain of quarters spewed out of the tiny, overloaded coin box onto the floor. PONG had been so successful that people had actually broken it by playing it too much. Nolan was in business.

He started his own company and began manufacturing PONG games and shipping them all over the country. Almost overnight, his games became nationally known and in great demand. Nolan and his company became famous. What was his company's name?

Atari.

Scott Adams, the inventor of exciting computer "Adventure" games.

6

ELECTRONIC
ADVENTURE

IN THE EARLY 1970s, Garry Gigax created a new kind of game that people played without using a game board. Each player acted out the part of a fictional character in the game. Together, the players embarked on a dangerous journey through a world they created from their imagination. The name of the game was Dungeons & Dragons™, and by the late 1970s it was so popular among young people that it had become something of a national craze.

Scott Adams was one of the early Dungeons & Dra-

An advertisement for one of Scott Adams' computer games.

gons enthusiasts. Scott was a computer programmer and a veteran of many years of playing Spacewar-type games on big computers. Scott decided to create a computer game modeled after Dungeons & Dragons. He called his game Adventure. When he started advertising it in computer magazines, he was swamped by requests for copies of Adventure for home computers.

Scott went on to found his own adventure-game factory, Adventure International. Scott and his company have also begun creating interactive novels, in which you get to play one of the novel's characters, then shape the plot as you go.

7

THE BIRTH OF A STAR CASTLE

WYNN BAILEY IS an electrical engineer who got his start designing computer cameras that could take pictures of people's bodies. In the mid-1970s, Bailey saw the first arcade games. He wanted to design games of his own. He quit his job and went to work for Cinematronics, a small company that in 1976 developed an arcade version of Spacewar that was the most sophisticated arcade game up to that time.

Scott Boden is a shy, twenty-year-old computer programmer. Boden works with Bailey to design new arcade games. Boden is a wizard at taking Bailey's game ideas and teaching them to a computer.

One day, Bailey approached Boden with an idea for a new arcade game. To get Boden started, Bailey took him into a room with a large blackboard. Bailey grabbed a piece of chalk and drew a star castle floating in the deep blackness of outer space. In the center of the castle was a huge cannon. Bailey drew circles around the castle. The circles were energy rings projected by the castle's defenders. The rings were to the star castle what walls and moats were to ancient castles on the earth.

Out in space, out past the last energy ring, Bailey drew a little white triangle. This, he told Boden, was the arcade gamer's spaceship. The gamer's mission was to blast through the layers of energy rings, destroy the cannon, and blow up the star castle.

Boden studied Bailey's drawing. The game looked too easy. The gamer could use two buttons (LEFT and RIGHT) and point his spaceship at the energy rings. Then he could push the FIRE button and blast right through them and smash the castle. It looked like a snap.

Then, with a twinkle in his eye, Bailey explained the rest of the game. Boden gradually learned Bailey's master plan for the game. He discovered that the game would be a terrific challenge. It would be hard to beat. But it would be exciting.

Boden returned to his computer typewriter and picture screen. He began typing game instructions to his computer. He translated Bailey's ideas into orders for the computer to obey. Some commands told the computer to draw the picture of the star castle, the rings, and the cannon. Others told the computer to draw the spaceship and make it respond to the buttons on the front of the game. Still others told the computer to make explosions, whines, beeps, and other sound effects to accompany the game. But most of the commands were a computer version of Bailey's game plan—the computer's arsenal of weapons to blow up the spaceship and defeat the person playing the game.

BEWARE OF THE SMART MINES

What are some of the weapons in this arsenal? Why is Bailey's Star Castle game so difficult to beat?

First, the star castle's cannon doesn't just stand still.

Instead, it rotates, so your spaceship has to keep moving, too. If it doesn't, the cannon will shoot the ship down the moment a hole opens in the energy rings. One blow from the cannon is fatal. And the cannon never misses.

And watch out for the *smart energy mines*. When Bailey showed these to Boden, he took the chalk and drew Xs on the outer energy ring. Each X represents a smart mine with the destructive power of a nuclear bomb. As it spins, the ring forms the mines, then flings them out into space.

Why are the mines "smart"? As soon as the mines leave the ring, they begin searching for your spaceship. They quickly find you and, glowing like fuses on a stick of dynamite, they fly toward you. If they touch you, you explode and disappear.

There's no escape. You can dodge and weave across the screen. You can press the THRUST button and blast around at high speed. But the smart mines don't give up. And they never lose your track. They keep coming closer and closer.

What can you do?

Fortunately, you have three spaceships. If the smart mines get your first ship, you still have two more.

Even better, if you can shoot the mines while they are still attached to the energy ring, you can destroy them before they destroy you. Also, if you are a crack shot, you can blast them as they close in on you in deep space.

As tricky as the mines are, they must behave the way Boden taught them when he fed the computer brain the game rules that control them.

It looks like the mines always know where you are. But that would have been a costly tactic. Your ship can move to a new spot on the game screen every thirty-eighth of a second. For a dozen mines to keep track of you, the star castle game would have needed more circuits, memory, and brainpower. Thirty-eight times a second, the little computer brain would have had to track you down and then tell each mine your new location. This would have made the star castle game too complicated and too expensive.

So the mines don't know where you are. Instead they fake it. Like prison guards patrolling a prison wall, they follow little patterns around the screen, searching for you. If you pay close attention, you can learn these patterns. Then, like a prisoner, you can take advantage of the pattern. You wait for the mines to head in one direction, then you go the other way. Meanwhile, you keep blasting the energy rings, and keep out of the cannon's deadly line of fire.

8

THE VIDEO WARRIORS

FIFTEEN-YEAR-OLD videonaut Steve Juraszek slipped quietly into the One Stop Beyond, an arcade in Arlington Heights, Illinois. Steve reached in his pocket and calmly pulled out a quarter. Like a gladiator stalking a lion, Steve approached a tall, brightly painted wooden box with a big TV screen stuffed inside a hole scooped out of the front. The box was Steve's opponent. Its name was Defender.

Steve pressed his quarter into the machine. His spaceship appeared on the screen. Steve hit the THRUST button. His mission had begun! Steve smiled, but inside he was coiled like a rattlesnake ready to strike.

The screen was filled with attacking ships. Steve was no longer on the earth. He had entered an outer-space world of high-speed chases, desperate rescues, and hordes of crazed aliens launching kamikaze attacks.

Steve played like a man possessed. He blasted across a jagged terrain that resembled shark's teeth. He blew up hundreds of aliens, reversed his direction countless times, and rescued dozens of stranded humans in bold, daring raids on alien bases.

After a couple of hours, the manager of the game arcade noticed that Steve was playing an incredible game, perhaps a record-setting one. He phoned Steve's mother and told her that the arcade would stay open all night. He wouldn't close the doors until Steve's last ship was blasted off the screen.

People gathered around Steve, cheering him on. Hour after hour, Steve continued to play. His victories mounted. A dozen more humans were rescued. A hundred more aliens were blasted to smithereens. Like a marathoner, Steve was using huge quantities of energy to keep up his ferocious concentration. To keep him going, people fed him pizzas and cokes. Steve chewed and swallowed. Then he scored another hundred thousand points.

The tension mounted. Steve kept playing through the night—ten hours, thirteen, fourteen, fifteen. Steve looked exhausted. His face was grim, reflecting the yellows and oranges from the video screen. How long could he survive?

SPLAT! Steve's last ship was blasted out from under him. Steve mumbled a weak insult, but the arcade room erupted in a huge cheer. People slapped Steve on the back and congratulated him. Steve looked at the clock on the wall. He couldn't believe it. He had been on the machine for an incredible 16 hours and 34 minutes.

Weary, his eyes glazed, Steve then looked at his score: almost sixteen million points. He had set a new world's record!

THE PATTERN MASTERS

Looking like a wrestler, Ken Uston stalked into a game arcade. He smiled at the manager, but the man gave him a look that reminded Ken of a crumpled top of a garbage can. Something between a frown and a cringe.

Ken looked for the Pac-Man machine. He walked over, popped in a quarter, and began to play.

The manager walked up and looked over Ken's shoulder. He watched Ken's little yellow "mouth man" being pursued by multicolored, hungry monsters. Every time the mouth man was about to be eaten, it made a miraculous escape or gobbled a power point. Then it spun around and began feasting on its pursuers.

The arcade owner looked at Ken. Ken was smiling. He wasn't even working up a sweat. The man shook his head, his frown drooping to his elbows. Quietly, he slipped away.

Ken is a pattern master. He is barred from gambling parlors and game arcades around the world because he can look at a game and, within moments, figure out a pattern—a game strategy—to beat it.

Many betting games, including blackjack, poker, and roulette, are games of fortune, luck, or chance. But even luck obeys some rules, and Ken has mastered those rules. He can't win every time he plays, but he wins often enough to make millions of dollars.

Computer games, too, are games of chance. But they are also based on computer programs—lists of instructions to the computer. Even the most complicated program eventually repeats itself. When it does, a pattern is born. Ken can spot that pattern and then use it against the machine. When Ken sees a pattern about to form, he can predict what the machine will do next. This gives him a chance to escape from a tight situation or score thousands of new points.

Ken and other pattern masters have written books describing the patterns they have found in popular computer games. Millions of game players around the world have read these books and learned the patterns. They regularly march into game arcades and get fantastic scores on machines whose patterns they have mastered.

You can learn these patterns, too. Once you have, the machine is beaten.

BEWARE OF VITAMIN CHIPS!

When the first pattern books appeared, arcade managers and computer game companies despaired. Eight-year-old kids were scoring hundreds of thousands of points on their best, most challenging games. As the kids got better and better, they played longer and longer on a single quarter. The flood of quarters from kids' pockets soon dried to a trickle.

Then the electronics wizards at the games companies got a bright idea. How about vitamin pills to perk up their games?

What sort of vitamin pill can turn a pussycat into a lion? Actually, the pill is really a computer chip, a tiny sliver of electrical circuits. The circuits contain a new game program. The game program makes the arcade game faster and harder to beat. It changes the rules of play. Even worse, it doesn't follow the old game patterns. If you try following one, you'll get clobbered.

Imagine that you are in your favorite arcade playing a fast game of Scorpion Wars. The action slows down for a moment. You look over your shoulder and see a woman enter the games arcade. The woman is all dressed up, like she is on the way to a company board meeting. She is carrying a brown briefcase.

She says hello to the game manager and then walks over to Planet Gobbler, one of your favorite game machines. She grabs it with both hands and whirls it around on its caster wheels, so that its front is facing the wall. She unfastens the back wall of the machine, and you can see its insides—wires, picture tube, and lots of aluminum shelves and bolts.

The woman opens her briefcase. Inside, resting on beds of white styrofoam, you see dozens of tiny computer chips, all arranged in neat, orderly lines. The chips are packaged in black plastic cases. With their hundreds of golden legs, they look like an army of Amazon beetles.

The woman picks up a pair of tweezers and carefully removes a chip from inside the arcade game. She replaces it with a chip from her briefcase. A moment later, the machine is back in place and the woman is gone.

You finish playing Scorpion Wars and walk over to Planet Gobbler. Curious, you pop in a quarter. This is a game you have mastered. You know all the patterns and routinely pile up mountains of points.

But not any more. This isn't the tired old machine you're used to beating. Now the villains—the planet gobblers—move like whirlwinds, threatening, blasting, and devouring. They are faster, smarter, and trickier. The old patterns don't work. The monsters move in new patterns. And you don't know a single one.

What did the woman do?

The new chip the woman plugged into the machine contains a new computer program stored in its tiny memory cells. The program replaces the one that used to control the machine. The new program has different rules, is more complicated, and runs twice as fast as the older program.

The new program makes the game much harder to beat. You can hardly believe you were once a high-scoring Planet Gobbler ace. Now you feel more like a green beginner.

But there's hope.

A week later, a new game book comes out that reveals the patterns inside the new Planet Gobbler chip. You learn the patterns and race back to the games arcade. After a couple of dollars, you start feeling like an expert again.

Even so, every few minutes you look nervously over your shoulder for a well-dressed woman with a brown briefcase.

Part III

ENGINES
TO MAKE
NUMBERS
FLY

9

THE IMPOSSIBLE DREAM

I wish to God these calculations had been carried out by steam.

Charles Babbage (1820)

CHARLES BABBAGE WAS an eccentric British mathematician living in London in the first half of the nineteenth century. He spent much of his time waging a vigorous war against London's organ grinders, since he claimed that whenever an organ grinder played, his ideas disappeared. He also wrote letters to poets and artists, scolding them for works that were mathematically "false or imperfect."

Once, when Babbage was still a young man, a friend caught him staring off into space. "Well, Babbage," the friend asked, "what are you dreaming about?" Babbage pointed to some tables of numbers and replied, "I am thinking that all these tables might be calculated by machinery."

Babbage tried to turn his dream into reality. He began designing a machine that would replace the army of clerks who hand-calculated and copied tables of numbers used by scientists, engineers, and ship navigators. Babbage's goal was a machine that could handle all calculations from start to finish.

Babbage ended up devoting his entire life and private fortune to this "mad, gallant" quest. Babbage's invention—the Analytical Engine—was never completed. The technology of the time was too primitive and his ambitions too grand. Yet his accomplishment was supreme: Charles Babbage had designed the first modern computer.

During most of Babbage's life, few people understood what he was building. It wasn't just that his machines were complex. People had built all sorts of complicated machines. They had even built calculators. But no one before had ever seriously tried to build a thinking machine.

THE DIFFERENCE ENGINE

Babbage's first machine, the Difference Engine, was to be a fancy calculator, not a true thinking machine. But the Difference Engine differed from all other calculators. It was to be automatic. After a person pulled the crank, the engine guided a calculation through several steps and then automatically printed its answer.

Unfortunately, Babbage's Difference Engine was never completed. He couldn't seem to finish what he started. Before Babbage completed one machine, he had already begun tearing it apart and starting work on a new, improved model. Also, Babbage was a loud, opinionated person who fought with his workmen, his colleagues, and his family. He even fought with the

This is a section of Babbage's first machine, the Difference Engine.

British government, which gave him money for his engines.

But the real problems Babbage faced were even more serious. Babbage had grossly underestimated the amount of work it would take to complete the Difference Engine. Even more damaging, Babbage was too far ahead of his time. Many of the parts Babbage needed for his engines still hadn't been invented. He had to invent new tools and devices, just so he could complete certain parts of his engine. Also, building a machine on the scale Babbage desired would have cost him fifty times more than he estimated.

Babbage's wife and several of his children died. His

funds from the British government dried up. Babbage's chief engineer walked out on him and took all of Babbage's specially designed tools.

Babbage had every reason to give up. Instead, he started work on a new engine.

THE ANALYTICAL ENGINE

Babbage calculated that his new machine would perform arithmetic at the unheard-of rate of sixty additions per minute. It would be able to solve any kind of arithmetic problem. The laws of thought would

This is part of Babbage's Analytical Engine. In concept, his machine was the first true computer. However, it was never completed.

The big device on the left with the dials is Herman Hollerith's Tabulating Machine. Sitting on the machine is Hollerith's card-punching machine. The device on the right sorted all the punched cards into the proper alphabetical or numerical order.

be built into its gears and pulleys. Babbage called his new machine the Analytical Engine.

Babbage conceived of the Analytical Engine a hundred years before the first modern computer was actually built. Yet he anticipated many of the computer's features.

Babbage's drawings described a huge machine composed of dozens of columns of metal gears, levers, and wheels. Yet the engine had only four parts. It kept important numbers needed in the calculations in a section called the *store*. It had a *mill* for performing the calculations. It had a series of gears and levers for transferring numbers back and forth between the mill and the store. It had a special section devoted to entering numbers into the engine and for printing them out.

Today's modern computers are far more complex than Babbage's Analytical Engine. Yet they still have only four parts. They have a *memory* for storing information (Babbage's store). They have a *processor* that controls the computer, performs arithmetic, and makes decisions (Babbage's mill). They have a *bus* to let the different parts of the computer, such as the processor and the memory, communicate with each other. And they have *input/output* (or "I/O") devices such as printers, TV screens, and typewriters, so you can enter information into the machine and get information out. These devices are just fancy, modern-technology versions of devices included in Babbage's Analytical Engine.

Babbage was never able to complete either his Difference Engine or his Analytical Engine. Yet, because of his engines, he still played a key part in the development of the modern computer. Today he is known as the "father of the computer."

Future scientists were blessed with more technical and financial support, and a more advanced technology, allowing them to eventually realize Babbage's dream. In 1944, Howard Aiken finished building the Mark I, the world's first significant modern computer. A short while later, in a magazine interview, Aiken admitted that: "If Babbage had lived seventy-five years later, I would have been out of a job."

10

AND THE COMPUTER WENT CLICKETY-CLACK

THOMAS J. WATSON, SR. was the founder and the first president of IBM, the world's largest computer company. Back in the 1930s, when IBM was just getting started, there were no computers. But one day, Watson heard about a man named Howard Aiken. Aiken, a professor at Harvard University, wanted to build an automatic calculator along the lines developed by Charles Babbage. The machine would be able to perform arithmetic and manipulate complicated formulas far faster than a human being or any other machine.

Watson arranged a meeting with Aiken and was impressed. Aiken was enthusiastic and seemed to know how to build his machine. Watson was convinced that Aiken, with enough backing, could produce the kind of

Tom Watson, Sr., the founder of IBM.

machine he wanted to build. Even more impressive, Aiken claimed that machines, such as his Mark I, would someday become as popular as typewriters in all modern offices.

Watson was proud of the way IBM had led the way in new office machines. If Aiken was right, and the Mark I represented the new wave of office technology, Watson wanted IBM to be its leader.

From 1939 on, Watson generously supported Aiken's Mark I project at Harvard. He loaned him four of IBM's brightest engineers, he financed the project, and he got Aiken the parts needed to build his machine.

The Mark I, also known as the ASCC (or "Automatic Sequence Controlled Calculator"), was an enormous machine. When it was built, it filled an entire wall in the red-brick physics building at Harvard. According to one observer, when the Mark I was working, "one could go in and listen to the gentle clicking of the relays, which sounded like a roomful of ladies knitting."

Watson wanted IBM to be a leader in office technology. But the real key to Watson's belief in the Mark I was Howard Aiken and his enthusiasm for computers. Whom did Aiken credit for his inspiration? In 1944, when he proudly announced the completion of the Mark I, Aiken referred to his machine as, "Charles Babbage's dream come true."

The Harvard-IBM Mark I, the first real computer to be completed.

11

FASTER AND FASTER

SEYMOUR CRAY IS a brilliant scientist. His specialty is designing fast, new computers.

In the mid-1950s Cray worked for Sperry Rand Corporation's Univac computer division. But in 1957, at the age of thirty-one, Cray and a number of other top employees left Sperry Rand and formed a new computer company. Cray wanted to spend all his time designing new computers.

Cray and his friends named their new company Control Data Corporation and before long, Control Data (CDC) was in business making computers. Cray led the development of the model 1604, one of the earliest transistorized computers.

Older computers, like the ENIAC, ran on pickle-sized vacuum tubes. In the late 1940s, scientists at Bell Labs invented transistors. Transistors were the size of paper clips. Like vacuum tubes, they could route messages inside a computer. But they were smaller, cheaper, and much, much faster. During the 1950s all computers switched from vacuum tubes to transistors.

In the early 1960s, Cray and other CDC designers came up with the Model 6600, the first successful *supercomputer*. Cray's company was so pleased with the 6600 computer that they built him a private laboratory within walking distance of his home in tiny Chippewa Falls, Wisconsin.

Cray had designed the world's fastest computer, but he still wasn't satisfied. He wanted to build a computer that was even faster. He knew of some new types of electronic components he could use, and he had some new shortcuts in mind that would boost a computer's speed. At his new lab, Cray designed the Model 7600, a computer that was even faster than the 6600.

During the early 1970s, the Model 7600 was the premier scientific computer. Meanwhile, Cray kept working in his private lab and designed Control Data's superfast STAR computer, the replacement for the 7600.

It seemed Cray had everything: his own private lab, a large corporation to support his efforts, and satisfaction from having designed the world's fastest computers. But Cray was unhappy. He felt that Control Data was becoming too big. He worried that the company's focus was changing from building supercomputers for scientists to building regular computers for businesses.

Cray didn't want to build regular, business computers. They weren't fast enough. So, in 1972, Cray resigned from CDC and started his own company, Cray Research, Inc.

Cray Research completed its first computer in March 1976 and sold it the same month. Today, years after it first appeared, Cray's computer, the Cray-1, is still the fastest computer in the world. In fact, the Cray-1 is so fast that it has up to one hundred times the processing power of today's other big computers. Running full tilt,

Seymour Cray and his supercomputer, the CRAY-1.

the machine can perform 200 million arithmetic operations in a single second.

The Cray-1 has a unique design. The computer's six-foot-high brain is arranged in a semicircle with luxurious padded couches around the edge. The small size of the brain ensures that none of its wires will be longer than three feet. The closer the parts of the brain, the shorter the distance the electronic signals have to travel, and the faster the computer.

The machine's denseness brings speed, but it also brings enormous heat, enough to melt the entire computer if it were not cooled. Thus, the comfortable, bright-colored couches around the Cray-1 disguise a powerful refrigerator. The refrigerator keeps the computer at a nice, cool 68° Fahrenheit.

Scientists can use the Cray-1 to build mathematical models the way hobbyists build plastic-and-glue models of boats, planes, and cars. Then scientists can "run" these models, like you would run a movie, and they can "look at" the way a bomb explodes or the way weather patterns emerge. Like a movie, they can speed the action up or slow it down.

The scientists have made computer "movies" of global weather patterns, of people's reactions to infections, of earthquakes, orbiting planets, and erupting volcanoes. They can watch a month's weather unfold on the Cray-1 picture screen in only one hour. They can spend a few minutes watching a person's body cope with an infection that might take days or weeks to develop in natural time.

People can use the Cray-1 like a scientific crystal ball to predict things that have not yet happened or to better visualize and understand things that can't be seen any other way.

Most of the time, Seymour Cray lives like a hermit,

working furiously and alone in his laboratory in Chippewa Falls. In the solitude of his lab, he scribbles formulas and equations on pads of ruled paper and sometimes spends hours concentrating on a single design problem. Gradually he begins molding the shape of a new computer inside his head.

His new computer, the Cray-2, is what occupies most of his attention these days. In sheer processing power alone, it's a giant leap forward. According to Cray, it will perform half a billion calculations in a single second.

After the Cray-2, will Cray be happy? Probably not. Already, another computer is taking shape in Cray's mind—a computer with enough power to dwarf even the Cray-2. How fast does Cray think this new computer might be? It will perform, he thinks, a trillion calculations a second. According to Cray, "I do tend to look forward in my thinking, and I don't like to rest on my laurels."

Seymour Cray says that he gets the same pleasure out of designing a new computer that a composer would get from creating a new piece of music. Cray's urge to create continues, just as strong as ever. Now fifty-three years old, he is not slowing down. Instead, just like his computers, he keeps moving faster.

Part IV

ARCHITECTS OF THE MICRO WORLD

12
THE
ELECTRONIC
SARDINE CAN

VACUUM TUBES USED to be an important part of a variety of electrical devices, including radios and TVs. They were also used on the first generation of computers. They could act like magnifying glasses and make small electrical signals grow larger. They could act like traffic cops and route signals through the computer. They could also act like light switches and turn signals off or on.

Even after improvements, vacuum tubes had several shortcomings. They were large and slow, and they consumed a huge amount of electricity. Also, they grew hotter and hotter while working. Early computers were like ovens filled with thousands of hot glowing vacuum tubes. The computers needed fans or refrigeration coils to cool them, or their wires and circuits would have melted from the vacuum tubes' heat.

FROM TUBE TO TRANSISTOR

John Bardeen, Walter Brattain, and William Shockley were physicists working at Bell Laboratories in Murray Hill, New Jersey, in the late 1940s. They were all interested in finding a new device to replace the vacuum tube.

They worked with silicon and germanium, two elements that acted as semiconductors when subjected to electricity. Some elements easily carry electricity. They are called *conductors*. Other elements prevent electricity from flowing. They are called *insulators*. Semiconductors such as silicon and germanium are halfway in between. When special conditions exist, they conduct electricity. Otherwise, they do not.

The three physicists made a good team. John Bardeen was the group's idea man. Walter Brattain was the group's experimenter, or inventor. He had been building gadgets at Bell Labs for almost twenty years and had developed an almost uncanny ability to combine things in new ways and make them work. William Shockley, the third member of the trio and its leader, was an excellent scientific detective.

On the afternoon of December 23, 1947, just before Christmas, Brattain and Bardeen were working in the laboratory, experimenting with the germanium and a couple of gold-wire electrodes—metal bridges that carry electricity from one substance to another.

Bardeen got the idea that if they closely spaced the electrodes, they might be able to construct an amplifier. An amplifier takes a small signal and boosts it into a much larger signal.

Brattain placed the electrodes close together on a germanium crystal, and turned on the power. It

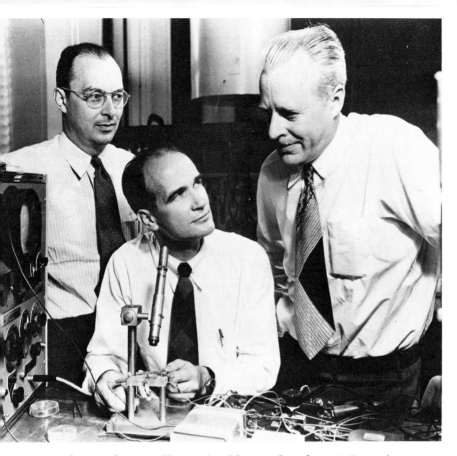

John Bardeen, William Shockley, and Walter H. Brattain (shown left to right) in the lab where they invented the transistor. The three scientists won the 1956 Nobel Prize in Physics for their accomplishment.

worked! Bardeen had been right. They had constructed a real amplifier. It boosted a signal right through a solid germanium crystal. The tiny electric signal going into the crystal at one end was at least eighteen times more powerful when it came out the other.

The three men called their new invention the *transistor*. The transistor operated much faster than the vacuum tube, and it used much less energy. The days of the vacuum tube were numbered.

FROM TOOTSIE ROLLS TO CHIPS

By the late 1950s, transistors were appearing in all sorts of consumer products, including hearing aids, radios, and TVs. But the biggest user of transistors was the U.S. military.

In the 1950s, transistors were the size of small Tootsie Rolls. The U.S. military, worried by Russian advances in electronics, was searching for ways to shrink the transistors. The military wanted to use the transistors in their electronic computers, satellites, missiles, and war planes.

The military funded numerous projects aimed at reducing the size of transistors. But it took two brilliant engineers, Jack Kilby and Robert Noyce, to discover that the best way to shrink transistors was to squeeze them onto a single *integrated circuit* (IC).

During this period, transistors were manufactured by growing a large crystal of silicon or germanium. The

The world's first transistor. (Notice the ruler showing the transistor's size.)

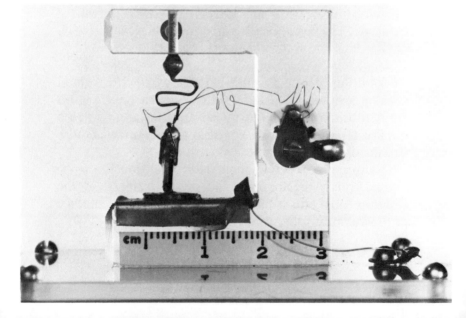

Three stages in the history of electronics: from a bulky vacuum tube to a single transistor in a protective can to a tiny integrated circuit that helps generate the musical tones on a Touch-Tone telephone.

crystal resembled a long Italian sausage. Next, technicians would use an extremely sharp buzzsaw to slice the crystal into thin wafers. Then they would install individual transistors on the surface of each wafer by hand. Last they would dice the wafer into many little pieces, the way a chef might dice an onion. Each little piece of the wafer had a transistor.

It took Noyce and Kilby to see the obvious: With all these transistors on the wafer, why separate them and reconnect them later into a circuit? Why not leave them connected?

In October 1958, Kilby, who was at Texas Instruments, connected each transistor on a wafer by hand and created the first integrated circuit. His idea was brilliant, but his handcrafted integrated circuit would have been a production nightmare.

At the same time, Robert Noyce, then at Fairchild Semiconductor, was also working on an integrated circuit. Noyce came up with a special technique to connect the components on an integrated circuit automatically.

Noyce's technique was cheaper, quicker, and easier than Kilby's homemade approach. It soon became the standard. In a couple of years millions of ICs were being manufactured and finding their way into radios, TVs, missiles, spaceships, and computers.

The IC gave a tremendous boost to the young computer industry. It had gone from using vacuum tubes to individual transistors, and then, beginning in the early 1960s, to ICs.

During the 1960s, computer parts kept shrinking. More and more computer parts were squeezed onto smaller and smaller integrated circuits. These circuits were like sardines, packed tightly together in a "sardine can" known as a chip—a square sliver of silicon the size of your fingernail and about as thick as one of your hairs.

13

THE
SHRINKING
COMPUTER

HOW DID COMPANIES fit hundreds of transistors on a chip the size of a cornflake?

First, a computer designer drew a maze of tunnels on a sheet of paper the size of a wall poster. These tunnels represented the chip's transistors and pathways for the electricity to follow.

Second, the designer took a photo of the chip, made lots of copies, and then took a final photo of a wafer of dozens of chips, arranged in a circle. All the chips on the wafer photo were exact copies of the original.

Third, the photo was reduced to the size of an actual wafer of silicon. The photo's negative was placed on the wafer. Using chemicals and light, the tiny tunnels in the negative were dug into the surface of the wafer. Each time two tunnels overlapped, a new transistor was formed.

When the chemicals evaporated, tiny specks of metal were left in the tunnels. These bits of metal would cause electricity to flow within the chip. They repre-

Ted Hoff, the inventor of the world's first microprocessor—a computer "brain" on a square chip of silicon the size of a baby's fingernail.

sented tiny gates and dikes to route electricity to different parts of the chip, as well as reservoirs for storing electrical charges.

When an entire wafer was completed, it was diced into dozens of tiny chips. The chips were tested. The chips that worked were packaged inside protective plastic cases and shipped all across the world.

THE FIRST CHIP BRAIN

Using these techniques, more and more transistors were placed on a chip. But no one thought about squeezing an entire computer brain onto a chip, until Ted Hoff, a young engineer at Intel Corporation in Santa Clara, California, did.

In the summer of 1969, Hoff was just out of Stanford University. He was working for Intel Corporation, a small chip maker. Hoff's job was to find a way to place twelve chips inside a desk-top calculator being built by Busicom, a Japanese electronics firm.

Hoff and his staff of engineers at Intel studied the Busicom design and felt it was too complicated. Hoff went to work and replaced several of the chips with a single, chip-sized computer brain.

The little brain was known as the Intel 4004. Almost as soon as it was invented, Hoff and the other engineers realized it could do a lot more than control a calculator. It could fit inside and control all sorts of other machines.

Chip brains created the first *intelligent appliances.* They were soon hidden inside automobiles, TVs, radios, watches, ovens, and dishwashers. A General Electric ad brags about GE's "intelligent appliances of the future." It features a starry-eyed customer walking away from a washing machine with a computer chip inside. The customer shakes her head and says, "I can't believe it! I just had a conversation with my washing machine!"

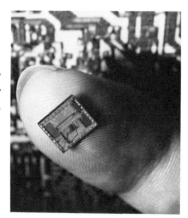

The Intel 8748 micro-computer—an entire computer on a single chip.

This **BELLMAC-32** microprocessor is as powerful as the "supercomputers" of a decade ago, yet it is only 1.5 centimeters long.

14
DO-IT-
YOURSELF
COMPUTERS

HERMAN LUKOFF HELPED build the ENIAC computer in the 1940s. He spent the next thirty years building new computers and watching the computer industry grow. He watched computers turn into a big business. Once computers could be built by a handful of dedicated men and women. Now they required hundreds of people, millions of dollars, and years of effort.

Then the computer on a chip appeared. New computer chip companies sprang up overnight. For a while, it looked as if new small companies consisting of a few dedicated employees could turn out powerful, chip-sized computers.

But *microcomputer* projects became as big and complex as projects to build large-scale computers. Robert Noyce and Ted Hoff recently complained that the new super chip from Intel Corporation, the iAPX 432, cost 100 million dollars and would have taken a lone engineer one hundred years to develop.

Gene Amdahl has been designing the world's fastest business computers for almost thirty years.

AMDAHL *VS.* AMDAHL

In the 1950s and 1960s, Gene Amdahl was IBM's chief computer architect. He was the chief designer of the IBM 704 in the mid-1950s, and, in the 1960s, he was Manager of Architecture of IBM's giant computer project, the IBM 360. Amdahl, better than anyone else, could dive inside a computer, dissect it piece by piece, and figure out new ways to connect the computer's brain and memory wires to make the computer more powerful.

Amdahl, like Seymour Cray, enjoyed being at the forefront of computer technology. Cray liked to design scientific computers; Amdahl liked to build the biggest, fastest, and most powerful new business computers.

In 1969, Amdahl left IBM because IBM thought his new computer idea was too risky. Amdahl started his own company, Amdahl Corporation. The new company's only product was a large-scale computer, the Amdahl 470. The 470 used the latest in chip technology.

The more transistors you pack into a smaller package, the more they heat up. An Amdahl supercomputer gets so hot it could melt. Gene Amdahl solved the problem by designing a cooling fin to dissipate the heat on each chip.

At first it looked as if IBM had been right. In 1970, the U.S. economy was in a recession and major companies such as Xerox, RCA, and General Electric were abandoning the computer business. They found it too risky and too expensive to compete with IBM.

What could a small, one-man corporation do against the industry giant?

Amdahl's new company weathered the bad times and built computers. By the late 1970s, it had captured one-fifth of the entire U.S. market for business supercomputers.

But in 1980, Amdahl resigned from his own corporation. Within days he had set up a new computer company he called Trilogy Systems. Who were its competitors? IBM, of course. And Amdahl Corporation. It was Amdahl (the man) *vs.* Amdahl (his old company).

Amdahl was fifty-eight years old and suffering from a bad back so painful that he couldn't get out of bed. Why was he starting over?

Gene Amdahl is a lot like Seymour Cray. He is happy only when he is inventing new computers. By 1980, Amdahl Corporation had grown large. It was under the control of outside investors, and it wasn't willing to risk leaping into any new technology. Yet Amdahl was not satisfied with merely keeping up with the latest technology. He wanted to stretch the technology and accelerate it even faster.

Amdahl has designed computers for every generation—vacuum tubes, transistors, and transistors on a chip. Now computers are entering a new era of the supersmall—the age of Very Large-Scale Integration (VLSI). VLSI stands for the millions of circuits that designers can now fit on a tiny flake of silicon.

Some companies thought that the old generation, Large-Scale Integration (LSI), was the limit to how small computers could get. The reason was simple. Each time you halve the length of an integrated circuit, you reduce the overall area of the circuit four times. Thus, you have only one-fourth the free space between the tightly packed transistors and other components on a chip in which to fit the vital connections. Experts in circuit design beat their heads on this problem for years.

Amdahl is not a chip expert. Yet he came up with a ridiculously simple solution to the problem. If the components are too densely packed to put in connections, he said, just make the chips larger. Then they'll fit.

Unlike many computer designers, Amdahl doesn't

think that we need huge teams of people to tackle complex problems. He was brought up to think that the individual makes a difference. He wants to spread that philosophy through his new corporation. He wants specialists, but he wants his specialists to climb outside their specialties and confront the big picture.

Amdahl wants to remain a creator and to build creativity and imagination into the lifeblood of his new company. He believes that you don't need experts to invent a new computer. You can still do it yourself.

15
THE NEW
PIONEERS

MODERN COMPUTERS LIVE in two separate worlds. There is the computer *macro* world. At this level, we look at computers as typewriter keyboards, as printers spitting out stacks of paper, and as sleek TV screens filled with words and colorful pictures.

But there is another world to computers that is many times more important than this large, everyday world. It is the *micro* world of computers—a world full of incredibly tiny transistors.

The micro world sounds like something out of science fiction. It is a world where microscopic transistors process information in a few trillionths of a second, where a circuit scalpel composed of a single wavelength of light is too thick, and where circuit pipelines are getting so narrow that electrons themselves might soon be too big to pass through.

Yet even as the elements in the micro world shrink to the point of disappearing, their importance grows enormous.

Most people are overwhelmed by the complexity of

these two computer worlds. They deal with this complexity by walling themselves off into narrow specialties where they can feel more secure. But there are a growing number of scientists and engineers who feel that a person can look at both worlds.

These scientists and engineers believe that even a college student can invent new computers to fit in the everyday world. But he or she must first journey into the micro world of miniature transistors. In this age of experts, it is very exciting to think that a young person can work in both worlds.

One person who teaches young people to be micro world pioneers is Henry Fuchs, a professor of Computer Science at the University of North Carolina at Chapel Hill. Fuchs is like a smiling human tornado, rattling and shaking everyone in his path. He preaches the new do-it-yourself philosophy of computer design like a minister preaches the Gospel. Like a good minister, he is gaining converts everywhere he turns.

Fuchs says that young computer architects should roll up their sleeves and start building new computers. They should begin at the messiest, most basic level—the level of the transistor.

Today there are layers and layers of chip experts, like the skin of an onion. These experts are the guardians of the computer micro world. When a computer architect like Henry Fuchs approaches, they shout, "*keep out!*" Fuchs is supposed to build computers from the chip up, not the chip *down*. "Leave the transistors to us," the experts cry.

But Fuchs has challenged the experts. He says that you need to look at the computer's goal. What is the computer's job? If you know the computer's job, you can build a computer especially suited for that job. It will run faster and more efficiently. You can spot

John Poulton (left) and Henry Fuchs (right) begin exploring a micro world by drawing diagrams and formulas on a chalkboard, arguing, and batting around new ideas.

shortcuts and improvements that would be overlooked by a chip expert who looks only at transistors.

Fuchs hopes to build a totally new computer. He will start by inventing totally new computer chips.

Fuchs calls his computer the Graphics Engine. He wants to use the engine to help his friend Ralph Heinz, a radiologist at the North Carolina Memorial Hospital in Chapel Hill. Heinz uses CAT (Computer-Assisted Tomography) machines to take pictures of "slices" of a person's diseased heart. Heinz would like to be able to take moving pictures of the heart in action. This would enable him to isolate the platelets, or fatty desposits, on the heart's vessels so he could study the role they play in causing heart attacks.

Present-day computers are not fast enough to give Heinz the detailed three-dimensional pictures and the animated motion he requires. If he bought a system for

Fuchs and Poulton use an array of computer terminals to design and test the microscopic circuits that will go into a new computing "engine" they are building on a tiny chip of silicon.

$30,000, all he would get is a picture of the heart represented as a frozen stick figure—what computer scientists call a *wire frame*. If he spent a million dollars, he would get a system that took pictures in color and three dimensions, but it still wouldn't capture the billions of bits of data and blast them onto the screen in real time. It wouldn't give him a realistic computer movie.

Fuchs feels that the choice for computer designers faced with trying to help people such as Ralph is simple. Either you keep trying to build bigger, faster, more expensive machines, or you leap into the micro world, re-examine the basic building blocks of computers, and try to come up with a wholly new computer that does what you need.

What Fuchs is saying sounds reasonable, but it is also revolutionary. If he and other computer architects are successful, they may completely transform computers as we know them. Ever since the 1940s, all of the millions of computers that have appeared have been von Neumann machines, based on the stored-program computer designed by John von Neumann in the late 1940s.

Now, Fuchs says, computer designers are putting on their work clothes and beginning the hard work of dismantling the von Neumann machine. Then they have to attempt something even harder. They have to build something better in its place. This might seem like an impossible task. On the contrary, Fuchs says, it is possible because he and his graduate students are already doing it. In addition, Fuch says, it's exciting, and it can be great fun.

CREATOR OF THE CREATORS

Lynn Conway is a computer scientist at the Xerox Corporation. She is co-author of the textbook Fuchs uses to design new computers from new chips. She says you get a special feeling each time you enter the micro world inside a chip. You feel like you are an adventurer

The computer created the "wire frame" head on the right by piecing together geometric shapes. Henry Fuchs wants his Graphics Engine to instantly create more realistic, complicated images, such as the head on the left.

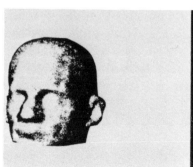
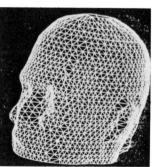

Lynn Conway is inspiring students and scientists all over the country to become architects of the micro world.

on an expedition that has set sail and has just landed in a foreign, unknown country.

You quickly become enchanted by the terrain—the mountains, the valleys, the uncharted rivers. As soon as your boat docks, you and all the others dash off the boat and begin exploring and mapping this new land. How much you find will be a product of your ingenuity, your efficiency in using landmarks, and your enthusiasm. But whatever you find, it is sure to be a surprise and unpredictable. Also, you can be sure that no one has gotten there before you. You all came on the same boat.

You are also like an artist creating something beautiful, new, and original. Conway says that she teaches her students—her computer artists—to look at the empty silicon crystal as a canvas, or as a blank slate, for them to do their art upon. She tells them to forget all the old rules and be creative.

She reminds her students that important new computers are no longer being designed just by the chip experts. Revolutionary new computers are being created by teenagers.

Young people in college are becoming computer artists and are creating silicon posters (enlarged drawings) of rainbow-colored transistors and circuits crisscrossing back and forth like a fabulous labyrinth or maze.

A student sends a drawing to a chip manufacturer. The manufacturer reduces the drawing to the size of a chip and transfers the circuits onto the chip's surface. Within a couple of weeks, the student gets the chip back, plugs it into a plastic circuit board, and attaches a power supply.

A close-up view of a micro world printed in silicon by one of Lynn Conway's students. The actual computing engine is only three-quarters of a centimeter long.

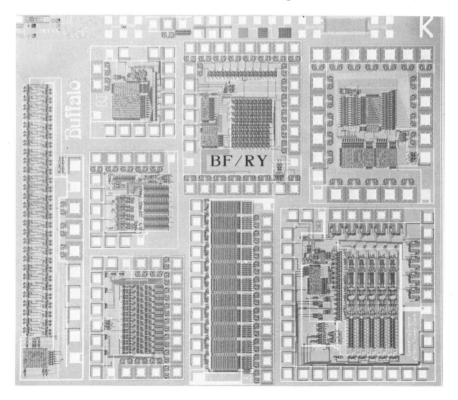

In a month's time, the student has designed his or her own computer. It might be unlike any computer in history. The computer might synthesize a human voice, spray a colorful, 3-D picture on a screen, perform some complicated arithmetic superfast, or process the images seen through a robot's video-camera eyes.

The image of the cold, humorless scientist at work alone in his lab is contradicted by pioneers such as Henry Fuchs and Lynn Conway. Their joy of discovery and enthusiasm are like beacons of raw energy that send new inventions and ideas rippling outward through our society. They charge people up to return to their labs and create their own new inventions and ideas.

THE CREATORS' MAILBOX

Conway, Fuchs, and other computer pioneers need to keep in touch with each other. What do they use to exchange messages? A computer—an electronic carrier pigeon.

For example, Lynn Conway at Xerox uses a network known as the ARPANET. This network is supported by the Advanced Research Projects Agency (ARPA) of the Department of Defense. It connects dozens of different kinds of computers together, enabling little computers to talk to giant supercomputers, and vice versa.

Using this network, Conway can hold computer conferences with fellow researchers and scientists scattered across the country and around the world. And she never has to leave her office.

Or she can send electronic mail to a colleague's electronic mailbox. Conway and her colleagues can share their new discoveries—at the speed of light.

Part V

THE
MACHINE
YOU CAN
TEACH

16

THE PATTERN WEAVER

ADA BYRON WAS the daughter of Lord Byron, the famous English poet. Ada was a passionate believer in physical exercise. She was a jogger.

Ada was also an accomplished violinist. Under the tutelage of the famous English mathematician, Augustus De Morgan, she also became a precocious student of mathematics. At parties, Ada often amused her guests by marching around the billiards table, playing her violin, and practicing her mathematics lessons.

On a trip to London, Ada once visited Charles Babbage's workshop. Other visitors were awestruck by Babbage's computing engines, even in their unfinished form. But Ada thought they were beautiful. She was able to understand, like few others of her time, the machines' engineering and their amazing capabilities.

Years later, Ada translated an article on Babbage's engines and added many notes of her own. Her notes are the clearest description we have today of Babbage's computing engines. According to Babbage, Ada's notes were the best description even he'd ever seen.

Ada Byron Lovelace, the world's first computer programmer.

Ada was thoroughly caught up in Babbage's dream. She was one of the first people to recognize that the power in Babbage's Analytical Engine lay in creating an automatic thinking machine that could be taught new rules and information.

Ada shared with Babbage the idea that many human reasoning processes could be expressed as numbers. Then she made the critical connection: once these processes were put into numbers, they could be entered into a machine. Ideas, thoughts, rules, and information could all be represented as patterns inside the machine. These patterns could be woven together to form new patterns.

Using a *program*—a list of instructions—consisting of these patterns, Babbage's machine would act as if it were thinking. The machine might not actually be thinking, but it would be going through the same motions, and the results would be flawless and swiftly delivered.

Babbage and Ada began a ten-year collaboration. Ada married Count Lovelace and had several children. Yet her partnership with Babbage grew more intense.

At first, Ada just looked over Babbage's shoulder and commented on his work. Later, she became actively involved and designed programs to run on Babbage's Analytical Engine after it was changed.

Each program Ada wrote convinced her even more of the machine's power and widespread applications. After a while she wrote fewer purely mathematical programs and began to think up programs to make the machine play tic-tac-toe, chess, and even music.

After Babbage lost his financial support from the British government, he and Ada concocted various schemes to generate new funds. The most famous scheme—and their last as a team—was a betting system to win money at the horse races.

Babbage and Ada, as two mathematicians, were sure they could figure out a way to predict the outcome of enough races to make money. At first it seemed they were right, because they won. Then they started to lose. The formulas they used to predict the races were not able to account for all the peculiarities of the jockeys, the racetracks, and the horses.

Ada's health began to fail. However, she continued to work with Babbage to try to raise money through the horse races. In her devotion, she twice pawned the Lovelace family jewels behind her husband's back. Twice her mother came to her rescue and secretly redeemed the jewels.

Her health deteriorated rapidly. On November 27, 1852, at the age of thirty-six, Ada died. But not before calling Babbage to her deathbed to give him instructions for paying off a particularly obnoxious London bookmaker.

ADA TO THE DEFENSE

In recent years, Ada Byron has been recognized as one of the major figures in the history of computers. In honor of her contribution, the U.S. Defense Department has named its new high-level programming language, "Ada."

The programming language was designed to head off a programming, or *software*, crisis. Programming languages are critical to a computer. They translate people's commands and their programs into the electronic pulses that the computer understands. In recent years, programs have become more expensive to develop, and they frequently are not very reliable, especially when they are long and complicated. The new language, Ada, will make it easier to program complex problems. The programs will be easier to write and will run more reliably.

Ada the person would be very pleased if she knew the progress that has been made on computers and that thousands of people around the world are programming computers in a language named after her.

17

DINOSAURS, BUGS, AND EXPLODING PICKLES

"ELECTRONIC COMPUTER FLASHES Answers, May Speed Engineering" proclaimed the headline on a front page *New York Times* article on February 16, 1946. The machine described in the article was the ENIAC ("Electronic Numerical Integrator and Computer"), the world's first modern electronic brain. (There had been other electronic brains before the ENIAC. None, however, was as advanced or became as well known or as influential as the ENIAC. The ENIAC is the granddaddy of today's *digital* computers (computers that use circuits that are either ON or OFF]).

In 1942, in the midst of World War II, John W. Mauchly, a physicist at the University of Pennsylvania, wrote a memo proposing the development of an electronic calculator that would calculate ballistics tables for the U.S. Army. The Army needed these tables to

J. Presper Eckert and the ENIAC, the world's first general purpose, electronic, digital computer.

determine the amount of ammunition required to fire its cannons and other big guns, and to determine the flight path of the shells fired by the guns.

For ten years Mauchly had been frustrated because so much of his scientific work involved making lengthy calculations with a paper and pencil, or using a slow calculator he had to operate by hand. Now he had the chance to interest people in building a high-speed electronic calculator. Mauchly called this new kind of calculator a computer.

Late in 1945, the Mauchly computer was complete. But it was too late for the Army. World War II was over.

Franz Alt was one of the ENIAC's first *programmers*. Alt thought of the other computers as "dinosaurs." Like a big brontosaurus, they were gigantic and enormously heavy. They were also slow. Compared with other computers, the ENIAC was like a whale. It was still heavy and big. Yet it was also fast.

Mauchly and other scientists realized that the machine, the ENIAC, was far more than a simple "ballistics calculator." Before the ENIAC, the fastest computer was Howard Aiken's Mark I. At top speed, the Mark I cranked out the answer to three addition problems a second. But the ENIAC, in just one second, could perform a thousand additions.

Why was the ENIAC so much faster? The Mark I used *relays*, little mechanical arms that had to swoosh through the air to send a message or make a calculation. The ENIAC used *vacuum tubes*. Vacuum tubes have no slow moving parts. They operate using heat and electricity. In a flash they can store information and route it around the computer. They made it possible for the ENIAC to increase its speed hundreds of times faster than the Mark I—even though it was built only two years later.

The BINAC computer, built by the pioneers of the ENIAC, was a binary, electronic, digital computer that obeyed a program stored in its memory.

Fast as it was, the ENIAC was still extremely difficult to program.

For example, you didn't just turn the ENIAC off and on when you desired. The computer had 20,000 vacuum tubes, each the size of a small dill pickle. The vacuum tubes were used as logic switches and signal amplifiers. Each time you turned the ENIAC on, two vacuum tubes somewhere would explode. It would take engineers anywhere from a few hours to several days to find the dead tubes and replace them. As a result, during the first year of its life, no one turned the ENIAC off. It was left constantly running.

You also couldn't get the ENIAC to obey a list of instructions just by typing RUN. Instead you had to think in terms of vacuum tubes and pulses of electricity. You couldn't feed your commands into ENIAC using a typewriter. Instead you had to manipulate the wires on a *plugboard*, a wooden or plastic board full of multicolored, spaghettilike wires. To get the ENIAC to solve a single problem you might have to fiddle with over a thousand wires on forty different boards.

All in all, teaching the ENIAC was like wrestling a giant caterpillar.

THE HUMAN COMPUTER

In the history of computers, John von Neumann is an almost legendary figure. He died in 1957 and his friends still recall the Hungarian mathematician's extraordinary quickness of mind.

Neumann's friends tell a story about a bright Princeton University mathematician who was working on a difficult math problem. The mathematician took a calculator home one night, spent most of the night struggling with the problem, and finally solved it.

John von Neumann, the architect of the modern "stored program" computer, standing in front of the IAS computer at the Institute for Advanced Study, Princeton, NJ.

The next day, von Neumann was walking past the mathematician's desk and happened to glance over the mathematician's shoulder. He saw the problem, but not the solution.

Von Neumann became immersed in trying to solve the problem. He began pacing around the room, mumbling to himself and nervously rattling and jingling his keys inside his pocket. The mathematician turned in his chair to face von Neumann.

After a few minutes, von Neumann's face lit up. He had the answer. "The answer is . . ." he started to say.

"51.734," said the man.

"That's right!" said von Neumann. "But how . . .?"

The mathematician left the room in disgust. Von Neumann had just solved in his head the same problem that had taken the man all night to solve using a calculator.

But von Neumann was glum, too. He was disappointed because he thought the other mathematician had beat him to the answer.

Toward the end of World War II, von Neumann was working on problems associated with the hydrogen bomb. As fast as he was mentally, he required some outside computational help. He went to Harvard and used Howard Aiken's newly built Mark I computer.

During the summer of 1944, von Neumann learned about Eckert and Mauchly's ENIAC project at the University of Pennsylvania. The ENIAC was to be the world's first electronic computer.

Von Neumann visited the ENIAC, learned of Eckert and Mauchly's progress, and began working with them. As a result of his work, von Neumann wrote two papers that acted as a computer game plan for the next thirty years.

THE VON NEUMANN MACHINE

Computers have changed enormously over the decades since von Neumann's paper, yet most electronic computers in operation today—from supercomputers to tiny pocket computers—are still von Neumann machines.

The von Neumann machine is a computer with a memory. The computer's memory stores both commands and information. The information inside the computer is represented as binary numbers (1s and 0s), rather than as decimal numbers used in the ENIAC. A computer's circuits all operate as binary ON/OFF charges of electricity. A binary 1 represents a charge of electricity inside the computer; a binary 0 means there is no charge.

Von Neumann's idea to use binary numbers enabled scientists to build a computer language that translated directly into the computer's circuits. It was ingenious. Now all the computer's operations could be directly linked to its binary, ON/OFF electronic circuits. This made computers much faster and more efficient.

Von Neumann also proposed that new computers be used for experimenting with *programming languages*, lists of commands the computer can understand. People use a programming language to teach a computer its jobs and tasks.

COLOSSUS, WHIRLWIND, AND THE BUG

In January 1943, at Bletchley Park, Buckinghamshire, England, scientists had begun work to develop a special-purpose electronic computer to decipher secret, high-level German military codes.

The code-cracking computer, called the COLOSSUS, went into operation in December 1943 and was a great success. Its high speed enabled trained cryptographers and mathematicians to crack the Germans' "unbreakable" code. By enabling the British high command to listen in on the German high command's secret messages, the COLOSSUS and its team made a great contribution to the Allied war effort.

Back in the U.S., after the war, the ENIAC's inventors spread far and wide. They organized new teams and built several new computers. One of the more interesting early computers was the Whirlwind, built at the

Captain Grace Murray Hopper at Stonehenge, England, in front of the massive stones of a prehistoric calendar "computer."

Massachusetts Institute of Technology (MIT) in Cambridge, Massachusetts. The Whirlwind project began in 1946, and the computer was running late in 1949. For a time, the Whirlwind computer was the fastest computer in the world. It was a monster. It filled a two-story building. It could do 20,000 multiplications a second, and it consumed 150 kilowatts of electrical power in one second.

By the early 1950s, modern electronic computers were processing millions of commands and billions of pieces of information. But teaching the computers was difficult. The early programmer had to translate his or her commands into long strings of ones and zeros. Then the person had to flip a switch to enter each 1 or 0 into the computer. It was no wonder that *bugs*, or errors, easily crept into early programs, and were so difficult to locate and correct.

One computer pioneer, Captain Grace Hopper, tells a story about the first computer bug. The first bug, says

Hopper, was not a mistake in some number. Nor was it an error of logic or arithmetic on the part of a programmer. Instead, it was a real live bug—a moth.

According to Dr. Hopper, while Howard Aiken and others were testing the Mark I computer at Harvard University, the computer began making mistakes. At first, Aiken figured that one of the computer's relay circuits had broken. After searching for a faulty computer part for hours, he and others located the problem. A moth had wedged itself between two electrical relays and had broken a crucial circuit.

After this incident, when the Mark I again started behaving oddly, Aiken and the other members of the team joked that the computer must have a "bug." As for the moth, it was pasted into the Mark I's logbook. Computer legend has it that the logbook is still being stored in a museum in Washington, DC—moth and all.

18
INVENTING NEW LANGUAGES

As EARLY AS the ENIAC, computer designers had begun searching for ways to get the computer to automatically translate a problem from human commands into machine, or electronic, commands.

Early programs used strange looking symbols and numbers. Programming a computer was like getting your teeth pulled: it was painful, it often required brute force, and it seemed to take forever.

John Backus of IBM was one of the most brilliant computer programmers of this early era. After several years of work, Backus and his team of programmers at IBM developed FORTRAN, the first modern computer language.

FORTRAN stands for the FORmula TRANslating system. Writing a program in FORTRAN is like writing half in English and half in algebra. FORTRAN automatically translates your commands into the ones and zeros—the ON and OFF electrical charges—that the computer understands.

BACK TO THE BASICS

In the early 1960s, the two major programming languages were FORTRAN and COBOL (COmmon Business-Oriented Language). Both were big languages with plenty of features for professional programmers, but not well suited for beginners or for people who weren't experts.

The way you programmed in FORTRAN and COBOL was very slow. To feed a computer your commands, first you had to sit down at a special machine that looked like a typewriter. When you typed your commands on the machine, it punched holes onto stiff manila cards the size of an envelope. When you finished, your program was translated into hundreds of little holes on those cards.

Next you had to take your cards to a window and hand them to an expert who operated the computer. Your cards had to wait in a long line for their turn on the computer.

Eventually your cards would reach the front of the line. The expert would feed them into the computer. They might get the computer to do what you wanted. But if you had a bug in your commands, they would not. Then you had to punch up some new cards and start all over. It might take days just to get the computer to figure out a simple problem. Working with computers required lots of patience.

In 1963, Tom Kurtz and John Kemeny, two professors at Dartmouth College, decided that there must be a better way for young people to learn to teach computers. Kurtz and Kemeny came up with a revolutionary new language they called BASIC (Beginner's All-purpose Symbolic Instruction Code).

Kurtz and Kemeny designed BASIC so that a student could sit down in front of one of Dartmouth's new computer terminals—a typewriter hooked to a TV screen—and start feeding the computer commands almost immediately. The commands in BASIC were simple and easy to learn.

Using BASIC, a student didn't have to type a program and send it off to a long line to wait its turn to run on the computer. Instead, as soon as the student was done typing his program, he could type the word RUN and press the RETURN button on the keyboard, and BASIC would grab the computer's attention immediately. The program would run, and if the programmer desired, it would even ask him questions and print out words and answers to his problems right on his TV screen or computer typewriter.

Today we are used to personal computers that sit on top of a desk or table. When we talk to a personal computer, we have its undivided attention. We are used to getting answers fast. When BASIC was invented, computers became much easier to use.

PASCAL

Niklaus Wirth and Tony Hoare are two famous computer scientists. Back in the mid-1960s, they grew discouraged trying to teach languages such as FORTRAN and COBOL to college students. They felt the languages were hard to learn and encouraged poor programming practices. Students' programs were ill-conceived and sloppy, rather than precise and logical.

Wirth set to work designing a new language that would be easy to learn and would encourage a good style of programming. He called his language Pascal, in honor of Blaise Pascal, the French philosopher, inventor, and mathematician, who had invented one of the first calculators.

Many people claim that Pascal will eventually be as popular as BASIC among personal computer users. They say BASIC lacks the tools to help programmers build programs that do what they're supposed to do and are easy to read. Pascal's rules encourage beginning programmers to develop good programming habits. Pascal programs run from three to twenty times faster than programs written in BASIC. Also, when you pull out an old Pascal program after not looking at it for a couple of months, you can still read it and understand what it is supposed to do. This cannot be said for most programs written in BASIC.

19
TAR PITS AND HIPPOS

IN A SENSE, a computer is like a giant onion. The outer layer of the onion is made up of computer languages like BASIC, FORTRAN, and Pascal. These languages are like United Nations translators. They translate commands in English into commands the computer can understand. People use the Englishlike commands to order the computer to solve problems, play games, and perform other tasks.

Inside the onion is another inner layer called the *operating system*. It contains computer commands that spring to life the moment the computer is turned on. They help the computer perform its chores correctly and on schedule. They help the computer manage its memory. They control the way information enters and leaves.

After operating systems were invented, people kept thinking of new jobs for them to do, so they grew in size. The inner layer of the computer onion bulged with hundreds, then thousands, of operating system commands. Unfortunately, these commands became so complicated that people who used the computer had trouble figuring out all of them.

Ken Thompson, the co-inventor of Bell Laboratories' UNIX computer-operating system.

Trying to use a computer with an overgrown operating system is like wrestling a hippopotamus: up close, it's too big and fat for you to see the whole thing. Also, it is too slippery to hold on to, and there is always the danger of being swallowed or squashed.

Ken Thompson and Dennis Ritchie are two very bright programmers. Ken and Dennis were working at Bell Laboratories in the late 1960s. Like many of their friends, they loved working with computers, but they hated working with operating systems the size of hippos.

For an entire year, between 1968 and 1969, Ken and Dennis disappeared into Ken's dusty, old attic. Using a teletype terminal that could "talk" over the telephone line with one of Bell Labs' big computers, the two men worked night and day to create a new operating system.

After months of unrelenting effort, Ken and Dennis emerged from the attic with a new operating system for Bell Laboratories computers. They called their system Unix. They took Unix back to their office, erased the computer's old operating system, and fed Unix into the computer. Then they let their friends and the other employees at Bell Labs use Unix.

Everybody tried it and loved it.

Unix is simple, so people with no training on computers can quickly learn how to use it to get their job done. Unix is like a toolbox. It has tools for expert programmers and for people just getting started. And the tools keep growing. When people invent a new tool they think others can use, they add it to the toolbox.

Finally, Unix is fun to use. Maybe this is the biggest clue to its popularity.

GETTING STUCK IN THE TAR PIT

There is a joke that programmers tell. The joke is about a doctor, an engineer, and a programmer arguing about whose profession is the oldest.

> "God removed one of Adam's ribs to create Eve," said the doctor. "A clear case of surgery."

> "But before that," said the engineer, "He created order out of chaos—obviously an engineering job."

> "Sure," said the programmer, "but who do you think created the chaos?"

Many people think that by buying a computer, they will make their company more efficient. Often, the opposite is true. A popular computer poster reads: "To err is human, but to really mess things up, you need a computer."

Computers often cause problems because they are complicated machines. They are complicated to invent, to build, to teach, and to use. Once they work properly, they move like whirlwinds. The problem is getting them to work properly.

Take the case of the IBM 360 computer. The IBM 360 computer is the most popular, best-selling big computer in the world. It was first developed during the early 1960s.

The IBM 360.

Building the IBM 360 computer was like building the enormous pyramids and sphinxes of ancient Egypt. The 360 project took a decade to complete and cost IBM over five billion dollars.

The 360 cost far more and took years longer to build than its creators ever dreamed. Why? Because of the software—the computer programs. One thousand highly paid computer programmers all worked together to turn out the 360's operating system. When it was finished, it consisted of almost *five million* commands.

Fred Brooks was the man who managed the development of the 360's operating system. According to Fred, software is the tar pit that traps computer designers, computer teachers, and computer users.

STOPPING THE MONGOLIAN HORDE

Western Union is the equipment arm of the American Telephone & Telegraph Company (Bell Telephone). In Lisle, Illinois, Western Union is building what is supposed to be the most advanced computer programming center in the world. Computer teachers in Lisle will write high quality programs to control the telephone company's electronic switching equipment around the world.

According to Dave Carnaugh, the center's manager, until recently there were no standards for writing programs, so each computer programmer used a seat-of-the-pants-approach and figured things out as he or she went along. This resulted in some pretty strange programs.

Nick Marselos is a young programming manager who works for Carnaugh. He says many programming projects still take the "Mongolian Horde" approach.

Frederick P. Brooks, Jr., one of the fathers of the IBM 360 computer.

You hire a horde of programmers and turn them all loose on the problem. Everyone attacks the problem, but nobody knows exactly what the problem is or how it can best be solved. Each person goes off on his own and writes a portion of the program without any idea of the program's overall structure or purpose. In the end, the program collapses from all its flaws.

Due to the fantastic growth in the computer industry, more and more programmers are needed to program more computers. The demand for programmers far exceeds the supply. Carnaugh is looking for new ways to teach computers. He is hoping for a breakthrough similar to the mechanical breakthroughs that sparked the industrial revolution. "If we don't solve this problem," he says, "we're going to wind up with most of the country involved in programming."

The key to the explosion in computers is their price. Computers used to cost millions of dollars. Now they cost a few pennies to produce. Their low price and small size have made them enormously popular. A flood of computers gushes out of factories. It flows across our country, pouring computers into one machine after another: calculators, digital watches, toys and games, household appliances, office machines.

We are entering a new era of intelligent machines. Soon almost all machines will have computers inside. But these computers must all be taught. If we can't find enough people to teach them, the computers will have to learn to teach themselves.

COMPUTERS THAT TEACH THEMSELVES

At Hughes Aircraft Company in Culver City, California, engineers sit down in front of computer keyboards and picture screens. They type into the computer the blueprint for a new product they want to build. The computer automatically draws pictures of the product on the screen, tests the product design for correctness, and then designs the product according to the engineers' blueprint.

The engineers and the computer work closely together. The engineers never have to teach the computer, and there is no need for a computer programmer. Instead, the computer programs itself.

Hughes Aircraft is just one of hundreds of companies around the world that is experimenting with new techniques called *program generators* or *automatic programming*. If these techniques are successful, they can be built right into the circuits of future computers. They will enable people to tell computers what they want done in a language like English, only simpler. Then the computer will automatically translate those orders into a program to get the job done.

Intel Corporation, one of the world's leaders in the production of chip-sized computers, has introduced a new, powerful, supersmall computer that has most of its programming built into its microscopic wires. Since programmers' salaries are going up and hardware prices are going down, the designers at Intel figure that it is economical to build sophisticated programs right into the tiny wires and circuits of the computer.

These new developments have led one industry expert, Robert Dalton, to write a report entitled "Are Programmers Really Necessary?" Dalton says that today's programmers are going to get a rude shock one day when someone with no programming experience walks up to them and shows them a program that was created automatically. According to Dalton, "Programmers as we know them today will be virtually extinct in twenty years."

20
PLAYING THE COMPUTER GUITAR

ARNO A. PENZIAS works at Bell Laboratories as a manager of research in electronic communications. He won the Nobel Prize for his discoveries in electronics and astronomy.

Penzias feels that in the field of computers breakthroughs are occurring so rapidly and so many new products are appearing that the average person can afford to be very picky about the services he wants his computers to provide. Arno Penzias feels that young people who grow up using new computers in their homes and in their schools will eventually arrive at universities, companies, and government agencies that use old computers. Then the two worlds of computers will collide.

Young people will be accustomed to using intelligent computers that act a lot like people. But they will be forced to use complicated, old-fashioned computers. Penzias believes these young people will create a terrific pressure on organizations to change from the older technology to the new.

Computers today are still not intelligent enough to behave like people. But the computer's great speed will hide its lack of intelligence. A great deal of computing power will be needed to do tasks that are simple for humans, such as talking, listening, seeing, and following simple directions. The computer will expend this power in less than the wink of an eye. Today's computer has the illusion of intelligence. In many situations, that's all we ask.

THE MOUSE AND THE STAR

Xerox Corporation recently introduced its Xerox 8000 office system, which features the Star video terminal. Managers and other professionals don't have to know anything about computers to operate the Star. In fact, they don't even have to know how to type. Yet they can create and edit documents, charts, graphs, and pictures. They can file and retrieve documents, and receive and send letters around the world electronically.

The key is a palm-sized device called a *mouse*. By steering the mouse and pushing its button, the executive can operate the computer. For example, let's say the executive wants to mail a document to another executive in a distant city. First she steers the mouse so that the little mouse arrow on the TV screen is pointing to a picture of a filing cabinet. She pushes a button, and a list of document titles flashes on the screen.

The executive points the arrow at the document she wants and pushes the button. Instantly, a menu of actions (such as copy, mail, print, or inter-office memo) appears on the screen.

The executive points the arrow to mail. An electronic address book flashes on the screen. Using the pointer, the executive quickly locates and selects the address of the other executive. She points to his name, pushes the button, and the computer tells her "The document has been mailed." Then it says, "I have updated the correspondence file to show you mailed the letter today." After this it asks, "What would you like me to do next?"

THE BEST WAY TO TEACH A COMPUTER

Computers have the ability to learn and remember new tasks and to do them over and over. This makes them unique in the world of machines.

We hear a lot about computers that understand human speech. We hear that soon we will teach computers the same way we teach a person: by talking in English or some other spoken, human language. Alan Kay, one of our foremost computer scientists, feels that much of the interaction between people and computers can be in English, but not all.

When the task is simple and straightforward, or when it is something we ask the computer to do often, we can give the orders in English. We might use English to tell a computer to turn on the TV, cook the roast, recall a phone number from a file, recite a poem, read us a letter or book, or summarize the evening's electronic news.

English is a poor choice when we want to teach the computer to solve a complex problem, draw a beautiful picture, play a new game, or manipulate information in a new and unusual way. For these tasks, according to Kay, "programming in English is the worst thing possible."

It takes years and years to master style, the rules and practices that help you communicate with other people. Yet, without style, it's hard to organize your thoughts and express them clearly.

When one person listens to another person, he assumes that he understands what that person has said. This is a bad assumption. Every day there are terrible communications breakdowns.

For example, imagine that a person says something to another person. When one person says something, the other person hears something else. What the first person says may be different from what he meant to say. What the second person hears may be different from what the first person said.

Confusing, isn't it? Much of this confusion comes from the fuzziness of natural language. It is a lot easier to be vague than it is to be clear.

Because natural language is not always a good way to think about and describe the world, people long ago invented artificial languages such as rhetoric, logic, and mathematics. According to Kay, "Mathematics notation wasn't developed for nothing. It has a crisp style. It is very precise."

Human beings are vague, ambiguous, and contradictory. For human beings, English is perfect.

Computers, on the other hand, like precision and clarity. They want everything spelled out, down to the last detail. For computers, an artificial language is perfect.

Many people have gotten very excited about computers because they require a person to feed it clear, unambiguous instructions. The computer doesn't tolerate lazy, sloppy thinking. Vague ideas get nowhere.

To use a computer properly, you first need to know the exact method for solving a problem. Then you must describe your method to the computer. Your description must be clear, precise, and divided into tiny steps.

Up until now, computers have always done what we told them to do. When they made mistakes, it was because there was an error in our instructions. But what happens when we rely on the new computers that obey instructions in English? Then we should get ready for computers to start making mistakes, doing the wrong things, and getting confused. In short, we must be prepared for computers to begin acting like people.

Or we can retain the artificial computer languages— those that are easy to learn and easy to modify and shape to our own purposes. When we want to build something new or important on the computer, we can use these languages in place of English.

THE ART OF COMPUTER PROGRAMMING

Programming a computer takes a lot of time. First, we write a program that supposedly solves a problem. Then we feed it to the computer. The computer may stop in the middle or do the wrong thing. This is because our program has errors. To get rid of the bugs, we have to study each command we fed to the computer to make sure it is right. When the bugs are all cleaned up, we feed the program to the computer again.

As we correct the program, something very important is happening. We are slowly coming to grips with the problem the program is supposed to solve. We are reaching a real, practical understanding of the problem for the first time. If we persist, we usually clear away all the cobwebs in our brain, and we clearly see the problem. As a result, we can teach the computer how that problem can be solved. If we taught the computer right, our problem is solved, and we have acquired some important knowledge in the process.

When we teach a computer, it is also teaching us.

The Turing Award, named after the computer pioneer Alan Turing, is the highest honor given to a computer scientist. Donald Knuth received the Turing Award in 1974 for his contributions in teaching computers.

According to Knuth, when we try to teach a computer to do a particular task, if the process is simple and obeys certain rules, then programming the computer is a science, not an art. It deserves to be automated.

However, if we sit down at the computer and build a program experimentally, not at all sure that our approach is correct; if we have to tear up our program and rewrite it; and if we learn a lot while we're writing the program, then programming is an art. Art is something people do much better than machines.

This means that writing the program is more important than teaching it to a computer. We can write programs to deepen our knowledge or sharpen our wits. We can write programs to give our mind a workout.

Knuth feels that one of his major goals as a teacher and writer is to help people learn how to write programs that are beautiful.

This puts the computer into the same class as a musical instrument like an electric organ or an electric guitar. A few years ago, "playing" the computer was painful and laborious. Only a few experts had the patience, background, and the training to use computers.

Today things are different. Computers are becoming instruments almost anyone can play. They can be fun, they can give us pleasure, and they can help us experience the world with heightened senses.

New computers will come with easy-to-use programming commands, light pens for "painting," electronic music, and a growing ability to "talk" to us and obey our spoken commands. How will we play the computer guitar? We will play it by programming it.

We should remember Ada Byron Lovelace, who thought of programming as the weaving of beautiful patterns. We should look at programming through Donald Knuth's eyes and see that:

> Computer programming is an art, because it applies accumulated knowledge to the world, because it requires skill and ingenuity, and especially because it produces objects of beauty.

Part VI

A COMPUTER IN EVERY BEDROOM

21
THE TRAIL BLAZERS

VANNEVAR BUSH WAS a brilliant scientist and inventor of one of the world's first computers. During World War II, Bush was the director of the U.S. Office of Scientific Research and Development, and his job was to direct six thousand leading American scientists to use their knowledge to help the Allies win the war.

Near the end of the war, in July 1945, Bush wrote a remarkable article in the *Atlantic Monthly* magazine. The title of the article was "As We May Think." In his article, Bush said that it was time for scientists to stop inventing the "cruel weapons" of war and start thinking about new peaceful inventions. Bush described the growing mountain of information in our society, and he called on scientists to devise new machines to help people manage that information.

In his paper, Bush came up with an idea for a new, general purpose computer that could be used by everybody. Bush called the computer *memex*. You could use memex as a combination filing cabinet and library. You could store all your personal information—books, records, letters, magazines, photos, and notes.

Memex was to have an enormous amount of storage. You could feed memex five thousand new pages of material a day, and it would still take you hundreds of years to fill memex's memory. All this extra space was critical. You could enter as much information as you wanted without running out of space.

But memex would really become useful when you tried to *retrieve* information, when you wanted to get it back.

Bush said memex should work like the human memory. Your mind does not work the way a book is written, taking one item at a time, proceeding from the beginning to the end. Instead, when you see something, you make associations with something else. You see similarities and connections. Memex would work the same way. You would tie information together by building trails through memex.

Let's imagine that memex has been built, and you are the first person who gets a chance to use it.

Think of yourself as an explorer. You are like Columbus preparing to set out on a voyage of discovery to new, unknown lands. As you proceed, it is impossible to follow a straight line. But you want to be able to remember the places you've visited and the things you've seen.

Memex does this for you. It automatically draws a map of your progress and records your zigzag trail. As you start looking through memex for important information, you see new connections to other information. That information may be scattered through several different books, magazines, newspaper articles, notebooks, photo albums, and so on. But it's all stored in memex, so it's easy to get to.

You investigate these new sources just by pushing a couple of buttons. As you search, memex builds a trail

Claudia Napfel's father built this computer out of spare parts
from several big computers. Claudia programs the computer
to play games and help with her schoolwork.

Herman Lukoff was a ham radio buff even before he helped build the ENIAC.

that ties all these sources together—including the notes you take that record your ideas and thoughts as you explore this new information.

Memex automatically preserves the trails of information and prints them out, like a book, at your request. Months later, you can go back to memex and call up and print out the same trail. It never forgets.

Unfortunately, memex was just an idea. But Bush predicted that a real memex would one day be invented. When the real memex appeared, Bush predicted the rise of a new generation of trail blazers—people who delight in pioneering new trails through the enormous mass of human knowledge.

THE THRILL OF PERSONAL COMPUTING

When Bush wrote his article in 1945, the first modern electronic computer, the ENIAC, was still being built. The ENIAC and the other early computers couldn't process and store the quantities of information Bush's memex required. After all, the ENIAC's memory could store only ten numbers.

Yet, even though the first computers were warehouse-sized monsters, their creators, the computer pioneers, saw them as personal machines.

As computers got bigger and could serve more users, the special one-to-one relationship between the pioneer programmer and his or her machine disappeared. But this relationship reappeared twenty years later, with the invention of the home computer.

Herman Lukoff was one of the pioneers who helped design and build the ENIAC computer in the 1940s. By

Lukoff uses his personal computer, a Radio Shack TRS-80, to help him run his ham radio station. On the right is Lukoff's "home-brew" computer printer—an old manual typewriter with solenoids on top of the keys acting as electronic "fingers."

The UNIVAC I computer. The UNIVAC I accurately forecast the outcome of the 1952 presidential election. This picture was taken on the night of the election. Presper Eckert, the UNIVAC's co-inventor, is explaining the computer output to Walter Cronkite of CBS News.

the 1970s, Lukoff was building big, modern computers. Hundreds of men and women helped him get each new computer on its way.

At night, Herman would return home and switch on his own personal computer—a Radio Shack TRS-80. Once again, Herman had an intimate, one-to-one relationship with his computer, just as he had experienced in his pioneering days. He enjoyed comparing the TRS-80 with the UNIVAC I, a computer he had helped build. The UNIVAC I was one of the first large-scale business computers in the world. "Would you believe," Herman said, "my microcomputer is more powerful than the UNIVAC I."

22
THE DRAGON, THE INVENTOR, AND THE APPLE

BOB ALBRECHT'S FRIENDS call him the Grand Dragon of people's computing. Bob started the People's Computer Company (PCC) in Menlo Park, California, back in the early 1970s. My wife and I visited the PCC in 1975.

I had been programming a top-secret military computer, hidden deep in the ground underneath the Pentagon. To get to the computer I had to flash four badges at soldiers guarding the Pentagon's halls.

Working on the computer was serious business. I learned to frown a lot to show people how serious I was. I got used to thinking of computers as "secret weapons" that were off limits to regular people.

Yet when my wife, Janet, and I walked into Bob Albrecht's People's Computer Company, there was a computer right inside the front door. Taped to the computer was a picture of a bright green dragon. The dragon was grinning.

Dozens of kids were climbing all over the computer. The kids were laughing and punching buttons on the computer's typewriter, making it spit out crazy messages and funny-looking pictures. The kids were playing games like HUNT THE WUMPUS, ZOT, MUGWUMP, and HURKLE.

Bob came up, grinning just like the dragon in the picture. He shook our hands vigorously and invited us back to see his "new treasure."

We followed Bob back to his office and found, sitting on a desk, the first personal computer we had ever seen—an Altair 8800. Bob surprised Janet and me by making a crazy prediction. He said that, before we knew it, thousands of personal computers like the Altair would be popping up in offices, homes, and schools all over the country.

Bob explained how he and his friends had started the People's Computer Company. He had persuaded Hewlett-Packard to loan PCC a minicomputer—a computer halfway between a giant computer and a personal computer.

As soon as it arrived, Bob brought busloads of kids in to see it. It was the kids' first peek at the exciting world of personal computing.

Bob and his friend, Ramon Zamora, have started an organization called ComputerTown, USA! Bob and Ramon are trying to put so many personal computers into Menlo Park that everybody in town will have a chance to use them. Bob and Ramon hope to get computer towns started all over the country.

Another project that Bob and others at PCC have begun is PCNET, a national computer network for people who have personal computers. To get on the network, you plug a device called an acoustic coupler into your telephone and computer. Using the coupler, you can have your computer call up PCNET. You can put a message on its "community bulletin board," or you can send your friends electronic letters.

MIND OVER MATTER

Steve Ciarcia is an inventor. He writes a monthly column for *BYTE* magazine, one of the leading magazines in the field of personal computing.

In each of his monthly columns, Steve tells how to build new computer-related gadgets: computer "watchdogs" for your home, "eyes" for your robot, or a low-cost "voice" for your computer. He has also described how you can convert a toy robot tank into a real robot.

Steve Ciarcia demonstrating an electronic circuit that enables him to operate a computer just by twitching his eyebrows. A circuit such as Steve's might enable a severely disabled person to use a home computer.

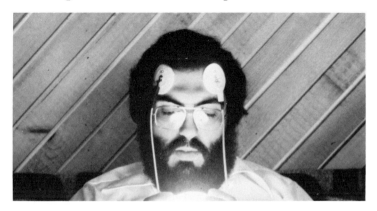

Steve has been fascinated by gadgets and machines ever since he was very young. He claims that he has filled several basements with his inventions.

Steve remembers that when he was ten, he rigged up a hidden wire on the bottom step of the stairway leading to the second floor of his house. The wire was hooked to his TV, upstairs in his bedroom. At night after his parents had put him to bed, Steve would activate the wire and then watch the TV in his darkened bedroom.

If his mom or dad became suspicious and started tiptoeing up the stairs to peek in on him, Steve was ready. As soon as they walked on the bottom step and touched the wire, the wire would automatically turn Steve's TV off, and Steve would dive into bed. Seconds later, when his parent looked in on him, Steve would be "sound asleep."

Today Steve still spends most of his time in his basement, inventing new gadgets. His tremendous curiosity sometimes keeps him up to four in the morning, trying to figure out some complicated new circuit.

Steve calls his current basement Ciarcia's Circuit Cellar. It is a fascinating place that looks a lot like the bridge on the starship *Enterprise*. There are video screens with floating pictures, multicolored wires draped across strange-looking machines, and computers playing electronic music and weird, eerie tones.

Many of Steve's projects have very serious uses. For example, in a column entitled "Mind over Matter," Steve described how you could build a computer circuit that would let you operate your computer just by twitching your eyebrow.

This might seem like a trivial project until you remember all of the disabled people who could use this circuit. A speech-impaired person who is paralyzed

Computer wizard Ciarcia in his "Circuit Cellar."

might use Steve's device to operate a computer or to send electronic mail. Or he might use it to activate a computer "voice" and, for the first time, "talk" to the outside world.

THE FIRST APPLE

In 1976, Steve Wozniak and Steve Jobs were college dropouts who lived in southern California and worked occasionally in electronics firms in the Santa Clara Valley. They had been reading about people building personal computers using the new chips. One day they decided to build their own computer and try to sell it.

To finance their project, they sold their VW Micro Bus and an expensive pocket calculator. With $1,300 in their hands, they bought some chips and other electronic components and withdrew to Jobs's garage. They worked feverishly for the next six months designing an experimental computer.

Once they were set on the design, it took them only forty hours to build the computer and drive it over to a retail computer store. The store agreed to try to sell the computer. Jobs and Wozniak were overjoyed.

After only a few days, Jobs got a phone call: the store had sold the first computer and wanted fifty more!

Jobs and Wozniak went back to the garage and, over the next several months, turned out dozens of new computers. Jobs is a fruit addict, so they decided to name their computer the Apple.

By the end of 1976, the Apple Computer Company still had only two employees—Wozniak and Jobs—but it had sold $200,000 worth of Apple computers.

And this was just the beginning.

Portia Isaacson forecasts a bright future for personal computer programmers, inventors, and entrepreneurs.

23
CHALLENGING
THE GIANTS

MANY PEOPLE TODAY feel that Apple Computer's success story cannot be duplicated. But there is one person who feels that opportunities for young computer entrepreneurs still exist. That person is Portia Isaacson. Portia has been referred to as the "First Lady of Personal Computing."

Portia has been working with computers for sixteen years. To Portia, personal computing means one person, one computer.

According to Portia, the personal computing industry offers some of the brightest, most exciting career opportunities for young people. Big computers offer opportunities, as well. But most programming for big computers is maintenance programming, in which the programmer is assigned to fix a program written by someone else. This can be tedious and extremely dull.

Portia feels that there is a great future for people who can program personal computers. She points to the millions of personal computer owners and their hunger for programs—game programs, business programs, science programs, and educational programs. She likes to remind people of the hundreds of programmers who are making lots of money by writing good, popular programs that people want.

Portia may be right. Hundreds of tiny companies are springing up all over the country. For example, in Chapel Hill, North Carolina, there is a new company called Med Systems. Med Systems is a software factory. Its programmers are some of the best in the business. They create adventure games, business programs, and statistics programs. They work with all kinds of computers and use all kinds of languages.

Med Systems has been in business only a couple of years, yet some of the programmers' games are becoming so popular that the programmers are getting wealthy. When I suggested to the president of Med Systems, Mike Denman, that he take a picture of his programmers for this book, he asked me kiddingly, "How about a picture with money spilling out of everybody's pockets?"

Mike's programmers are a diverse group of people. They have a wide range of interests and personalities. But they also have something in common: except for one college freshman, all the programmers at Med Systems are high school students.

DAVE AND GOLIATH

IBM, Radio Shack, Apple, Commodore, and Atari have cornered most of the market for personal computers. The companies are multimillion-dollar operations, each employing hundreds or thousands of people.

If you invented a new computer, do you think you would stand a chance competing with these giants?

Most people would say no.

But in Raleigh, North Carolina, there are two people who say yes.

The two people are Hal Chamberlin and Dave Cox. They have a new computer, and they're ready to challenge the giants.

Hal and Dave have been building computers for about fifteen years. Hal was one of the earliest computer hobbyists. In the September 1972 issue of the *Amateur Computer Society Newsletter*, Hal wrote about his homemade computer, the HAL-4096. It was an advanced computer that used an IBM typewriter to print out information. For $2, Hal would send people a complete set of plans so they could build their own HAL-4096.

In 1974, Hal and Dave founded Micro Technology Unlimited, a tiny company in Raleigh. For the last eight years, they have been building computer circuit boards, the green plastic cards that computer chips get plugged into.

All of the years of designing and building computer parts have taught Hal and Dave how to build a computer right. They think it is now time to start producing their own computer.

When the two men looked at the small-computer industry, they didn't see themselves as Davids going to battle with corporate Goliaths. They ignored the companies and focused only on their computers. They looked at what each computer could and couldn't do. Studying the other computers convinced Hal and Dave that they could invent a better machine.

Today, Micro Technology is still a small company. Yet its staff of about fifteen people are working night and day to design and produce Hal and Dave's new brainchild—the MTU 130.

Hal and Dave's new computer has been designed and

built by only a handful of men and women. There is no way of telling if Micro Technology is on its way to becoming another Apple Computer Company. Yet Hal and Dave have shown that individuals and a small company can still invent a new computer and challenge the giants.

Alan Kay is developing a notebook-sized personal computer that will play music and create animated movies and cartoons.

24

PUT A SUPER-
COMPUTER
IN YOUR
NOTEBOOK

MANY YEARS AGO, Alan Kay read Vannevar Bush's paper, "As We May Think," and learned about Bush's memex computer. Alan became fascinated with the idea of building a personal computer with the capabilities of a memex.

During the mid-1960s, as Alan worked towards his Ph.D. in Computer Science at the University of Utah, he began designing his new computer. Alan wanted the computer to be as powerful as the biggest computers of the 1960s. A person could use it to draw pictures, create computer cartoons, and compose music. He or she could use it to make phone calls to the world's largest computers and borrow information from their electronic libraries.

Alan had been a professional musician before going into computer science. He felt that music was an essential feature in a personal computer. He wanted the computer to be like a good musical instrument, both in its quality and in its quick response. For example, we don't like to listen to a piano that is out of tune, and when we blow into a flute, we expect music to come out the other end instantly.

Alan began building his new machine in 1967. Between 1967 and 1969 he designed an experimental computer he called FLEX. FLEX taught Alan that he had a long way to go before he could build the type of computer he wanted.

In 1970, Alan went to work for Xerox and headed a team to build his personal computer. Alan's team didn't want their computer to be based on the technology of 1970, but on the technology of the mid-1980s. By that time, computer chips would be available that could process information at a rate of ten million commands a second and store an encyclopedia in their memory. Alan and his team hoped that the chips of the '80s would enable them to build a supercomputer the size of a notebook.

The computer's size was important. A true, personal computer must be small enough for a person to carry anywhere. Yet it must be large enough to contain a speaker for music, a picture screen to show cartoons and messages, and a nice-sized keyboard for entering information and commands. Alan and his team called their computer the Dynabook.

During the 1970s, the Dynabook team had to work with current technology even while anticipating the technology of the future. They designed a desktop model of the Dynabook called the Altos. The Altos had a keyboard, a tall picture screen, a disk drive (to store large quantities of information and programs when the computer was turned off), and a pointing device called a "mouse."

Let's imagine that you are using the Altos. Sitting in front of you on a square board is the Altos mouse. It is connected by a wire leash to the Altos. By rolling the mouse around on the board, you can move an arrow on the picture screen. The picture screen shows a menu of things you can do on the computer—make a computer movie, conduct an experiment, or play music.

You move the mouse to make its arrow point to each item. To select an item, you push the mouse's button, and the computer automatically does the thing you pointed to. It might flash a picture on the screen, rotate a triangle, or talk to you in a robotlike voice.

The team also developed a new programming system to run on the Altos. They called their system Smalltalk. Smalltalk was easy to learn and use and powerful. By giving the computer just a couple of commands, you could get a lot done.

How does Smalltalk differ from most other computer languages?

Programming in most languages is a lot like baking a cake. You need to follow a recipe and add ingredients as you go. Similarly, to write a program, you need a step-by-step list of things for the computer to do (the recipe), and you need to add information (the ingredients).

Programming in Smalltalk is less like baking a cake and more like directing a play. You search through the Smalltalk program library and find some "actors" that are close to what you want. You have these actors perform for you on the picture screen stage, then you modify them and their routines until you're satisfied.

For example, let's say you want to develop a spaceship tag game using Smalltalk. Looking at the Smalltalk program library, you notice that there are some triangles that you could use as spaceship "actors." Also, you notice that the triangles can rotate and be moved swiftly around the screen.

You retrieve the triangles from the computer's memory. You slightly modify their shapes until they closely resemble spaceships, and you modify their functions to allow them to chase each other and escape.

WHAT IS A PERSONAL COMPUTER?

Don't we already have personal computers? Isn't Alan Kay's computer just going to be a little faster, a little fancier?

Alan wants to build a computer with three things today's personal computers lack: it must be small, it must be immensely powerful, and it must be easy to use.

First, small size. Except for the primitive pocket computers, most of today's personal computers are too big to carry with you. They sit on a desk or table, and they must be plugged into an electric outlet. They are not at all portable.

Second, immense power. Today's computers have limited memory and limited speed. Realistic pictures, movies, music, and speech require huge speeds and an enormous memory. Most personal computers today can store only a few pages from a book. That's a long way from an encyclopedia at your fingertips.

Third, simplicity. Most computers today are not really personal. The average person has a hard time learning enough commands to make today's computer do something useful. Many people buy computers, then get so frustrated with them, they resell them, junk them, or toss them into a closet.

In late 1981, Alan left Xerox and went to work for Atari. At Atari he is working on an even more advanced system than Smalltalk. It is called Rainbow. Rainbow is Alan's next step toward the Dynabook.

For Alan Kay, a notebook-sized Dynabook remains a dream. Yet, right now, Alan is still pursuing his goal of twenty years: to develop a portable, personal computer—a tiny machine filled with unbelievable power.

Part VII

PEOPLE HELPERS, SPACESHIPS, AND TURTLES

25
WHEELCHAIR COMPUTER EXPERTS

JOE VILLAREAL LIVES in an apartment in Palo Alto, California. He operates a mail-order business out of his apartment. His Apple computer enables him to manage the typing, mailing, researching, and bookkeeping of an operation that once might have employed several people.

Joe is excited about his new business because he had a problem finding work outside his home. Joe is unable to walk. He's confined to a wheelchair.

David McFarling runs his business out of his home in Lincoln, Nebraska. David is a computer programmer and an energetic businessman. He advertises and sells computer programs nationally. David does all his company's business and programming on his home computer. David is severely disabled. Like Joe, he is a wheelchair computer expert.

David types on his computer by raising and lowering his right arm and tapping the keys with one stiff finger.

He has no movement in any of his fingers and can barely move his left arm.

In the past, disabled, elderly, and injured persons were considered to be deadweight, socially and economically. Many people saw disabled persons as charity cases or as a drain on the taxpayer's dollar. The computer is changing this view swiftly and dramatically. Disabled people, persons with serious injuries, and many elderly people are acquiring small computers and using them to start their own businesses. Others do programming for large companies.

Still others dial up big deals on their telephones. The big computers form the hub of an electronic network of elderly and disabled people. They can use the network to take courses, get the news, or just communicate with each other. They don't have to leave home to do this either.

Telecommuting means going to work electronically, by plugging your home computer into a telephone. You sit at your computer and type in your work on its keyboard. The computer sends your work over the phone line to your company's big computer.

Telecommuting may become a popular alternative to driving a gas-guzzling car through rush-hour traffic every day. People such as Joe Villareal and David McFarling are already telecommuting all over the country, and in the meantime, running successful businesses out of their homes.

Computer programs for new, personal computers will be in great demand for the next decade, at least. People and companies are desperate for good programs, and computer programmers are in short supply. People who are homebound or confined to an institution can take electronic correspondence courses in computer programming. They can do all their work without leaving their bedroom. Even prison inmates can begin new careers.

In New Jersey, Phil Miller and Ken Greene have started a company called Avant Courier. Avant Courier trains disabled people to become computer programmers. It then markets the programs they produce.

Miller, Green, and others are now working with state government agencies to get their support for a statewide computer training program for disabled people. They feel the state should train people to support themselves doing computer programming.

26

AN
INTELLIGENT
ARM

TELESENSORY SYSTEMS IN California has developed a "talking" calculator blind people can use. In Cambridge, Massachusetts, Ray Kurzweil has invented a computerized reading machine for blind people. When a blind person places a book on Ray's machine, it scans the book and then reads it back out loud.

Another company has developed a computerized device called the OptoCom. A person who has lost the use of his arms and legs can get OptoCom to type a message just by looking at letters on a picture screen. When the person focuses on "A," for instance, OptoCom tracks his eye movements, realizes he is looking at the "A," and gets the computer to type the "A" on a typewriter. After some training and practice, a severely disabled person can use OptoCom to type quite rapidly—with his eyes!

At Carnegie-Mellon University, Dr. Raj Reddy and his colleagues have developed a program that under-

164

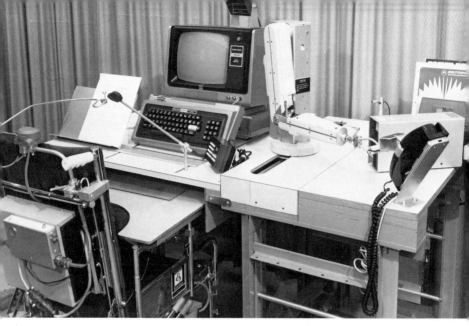

A person who has a spinal cord injury (and who cannot move his arms or legs) can operate this computerized robotic arm by jiggling his chin and sending signals to the arm via a chin controller mounted on his wheelchair. Using the robotic arm and sitting at this work station, the person can work on a computer, make telephone calls, and eat his meals.

stands human speech. Reddy calls the program HEARSAY. Programs such as HEARSAY will give computers "ears" and enable them to obey voice commands given to them by blind people and people who can't move their arms or legs.

Using a program such as HEARSAY, disabled or bedridden people can order the computer to type and mail a letter, tell the time, read a summary of the weather or news, sound an alarm, or control household appliances. They can do all this just by giving the computer a verbal command.

Several companies have developed computer typewriters with voices. When you push a button, the typewriter tells you what it has typed. Bell Labs has a com-

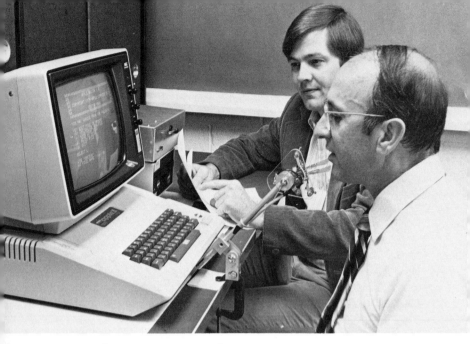

Woodrow Seamone (right) is using a device he invented to type a letter on the computer. Using this device, a disabled person can work on a computer by moving his lip or chin. Wolfger Schneider (left), the device's co-inventor, is dictating the letter that Seamone is "typing."

puter telephone that lets you dial just by saying the phone number out loud.

At Johns Hopkins University, Woody Seamone, Wolfgar Schneider, and Gerhard Schmeisser have developed an intelligent robotic arm. Seamone says that a person who has lost an arm can use the robotic arm to do things he would have done with his real arm, including reading and eating, or using a typewriter or telephone, or operating a personal computer.

The arm is controlled by a tiny, computer brain on a chip inside the arm. Even a totally paralyzed person can use the arm simply by jiggling a chin controller under his jaw. The chin controller sends a signal to the arm, which is mounted nearby on a worktable, and the arm performs the desired task.

M.A. Rahimi, of Wayne State University, is working on several forms of computers to help disabled people who have trouble talking or hearing. There are more than twenty million persons in the U.S. who have some sort of communications disability. Rahimi says that new, intelligent computers will work with people and translate even slight body movements or blinks of the eyes into clear messages. A message might flash on a

Mark Dahmke (left) watching his friend, Steve Rush, use the "Bionic Voice," a computerized system that Mark developed. Steve, a quadriplegic, can make the computer talk for him by tapping its keys with his head stick.

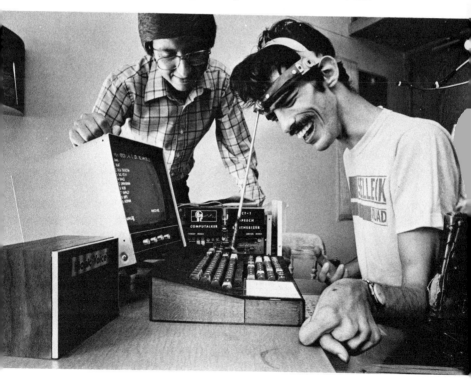

Mary Robinson is the co-developer of DEAFNET, a national computer network for hearing-impaired people. In this photo, Robinson is teaching deaf people how to use the computer.

computer display screen or be spoken aloud as a computer voice.

Smart computers and robots will soon be so cheap that almost every disabled person will be able to get one. When the person wants to play, work, or communicate, she will do it using her computer. With the computer's help, she will do things as well as anyone. The computer will erase her disability.

Today, most disabled people do not have computers. Rahimi says it is society's responsibility to put computers into the hands of disabled people as soon as possible.

27
FLYING SOLO

TOM DWYER IS a teacher and computer scientist at the University of Pittsburgh. He has taught computer courses at the university and at local high schools. Dwyer's most famous project, the Soloworks Laboratory, has been in operation since 1969. The project gets its name from Dwyer's goal of having every student learn things by flying solo.

Dwyer says in most classrooms, teachers and students fly dual. The student is a novice pilot and is always under the teacher's complete control.

In the Soloworks Lab, the teachers train students to take off and fly using the wings of their imagination. On their own, they explore new subjects, perform experiments, and discover new ideas. The vehicle the students "fly" is the classroom computer.

The Soloworks Lab has recently become the Solo/NET/Works Project and has installed a classroom network of small computers. A network is a group of computers all plugged into each other and talking to each other. On the Solo network, each student has his own computer. He can use the computer to send messages to other computers on the network. He and his computer can play games with the other students and their computers.

The student and his computer are like teammates or buddies. They compete together in network contests. They work together to complete classroom assignments and projects.

Margot Critchfield is an author, illustrator, and educator, who works closely with Dwyer and the new project. Computers, she says, can do more than process information or do arithmetic. She says a computer is like a chameleon changing color—it can change into many shapes. A computer can be taught to act like any other machine ever invented.

As part of their work on the project, students are asked to teach the computer to play the part of other machines. One machine the computer can act like is a

More and more high school students are getting a chance to work with small, desktop computers.

spaceship in a game called N-Trek. N-Trek is a version of the popular Star Trek computer game.

In N-Trek, the computer has been told to act like the starship *Enterprise*. Each student sits at a computer and acts as if he or she is a member of the *Enterprise's* crew, sitting on the bridge in front of a computer console. Together, the students operate their computer consoles and launch the *Enterprise* into outer space on missions of science and exploration.

N-Trek is what Tom Dwyer calls *inventive learning*. Each student has to write the program that runs on his or her console and talks with all other consoles aboard the *Enterprise*. During takeoff or exploration of a new solar system, the student has several tasks to perform. Some he performs alone. Others he performs in cooperation with the rest of the crew.

For example, during any particular flight, a person may have to cope with an emergency equipment malfunction, or an incident of food poisoning in the *Enterprise* mess room. Or she may use the computer to perform arithmetic calculations to load and unload some important cargo. Or he may need to plot coordinates on the screen to navigate the starship. Or he may plan with other crew members how to send a landing party down to the mysterious, potentially dangerous, planet they are now orbiting.

To perform all these tasks, the student must learn to be inventive and self-reliant, yet also be a good member of the team. In addition, he must learn to communicate his ideas and needs effectively to other crew members via the computer keyboard and screen. When an emergency arises, he must be able to find information in the computer's library that can save the ship or rescue a person.

Dwyer and his crew of teachers and students have

great plans for the future. They are going to expand their N-Trek game. They are also working on an air-traffic control simulation, in which students will play the part of air-traffic controllers and pilots of large airplanes that are trying to land and take off from a major airport.

Dwyer also hopes to organize computer contests between students in different schools. It will be a new kind of sport, like a football game or a soccer match. But the entire game will be fought on the computer, on lots of computers.

Imagine that it is a Saturday morning in the near future.

Four crack teams of computer pilots from four different schools are sitting in front of their computers. At the same time, they see the word "GO!" flash on their computer screens. They press some final buttons, power up their computer spaceships, and blast off.

Each team's goal is to be the first human beings to plunge through Saturn's rings and return safely to Earth.

As they work feverishly, the students' ground-based controller (their coach) reminds them to watch out for the asteroid belt between Mars and Jupiter. He warns them about the radioactive tail of the comet whooshing toward Earth.

Then he wishes them good luck, and they're off!

28

PLATO AND
SMALLTALK

DONALD BITZER IS a magician.

He can make coins shrink and eggs pop out from behind your ears.

If you ever work for Don, don't take off your shoes. When you go to put them back on, you may find they have become the home of a family of white rabbits. Don't be surprised if you see a baby chick peek out of your coffee cup too.

Don is a master of sorcery and magical illusions. But most people don't get to see Don wearing his tall, black magician's hat. They know him as a brilliant inventor and director of a computer laboratory at the University of Illinois.

Don is most famous for one of his inventions, PLATO. PLATO is a teaching computer. Don invented PLATO in 1960.

PLATO is an extremely fast and powerful supercomputer at the University of Illinois in Champaign. It teaches using a typewriter and a strange-looking TV.

Together the computer typewriter and TV are known as a *terminal*. The terminal's TV is a big metal box with a slanted *plasma-ray* screen on the front. The pictures

This photo of Donald Bitzer was created by his PLATO computer.

and letters on the screen are all in orange. The screen is one of Bitzer's many inventions. Unlike a regular TV picture-tube, the plasma-ray tube is flat. This makes it possible to pack many extra features inside a box behind the screen.

For example, inside the box is a filmstrip and slide projector. Based on a command typed in on the keyboard, the slide projector will flash a picture on the computer screen. The image might be a beautiful color slide of an animal the class is studying, or it might be a picture of a volcanic eruption on Io, a moon of Jupiter.

The terminal has many other features as well. It can talk, play music, and, under your control, produce a computer cartoon show, with cartoon characters you design yourself.

When you first sit down at the terminal, it puts a menu of things to do on the screen. To make your first choice, you just touch the screen and the computer instantly obeys your request.

Thousands of students have taken entire courses from PLATO. Each student works with his or her own PLATO terminal.

Teachers create their lessons by using a special course-authoring language called TUTOR. Even if the teacher is not a computer programmer, she can use TUTOR to create educational programs for the students that guide them through new material, evaluate their progress, and produce fancy effects with color slides, music, and animated color figures, maps, and diagrams.

Students using the PLATO system go on a variety of explorations as part of their learning. They journey inside the human body, they visit a beehive and learn about genetics and reproduction, they study the effects of overpopulation on our world's ecology, and they play games in which they act as managers of a large corporation.

Often, computers that serve many users at the same

The PLATO computer draws this picture on the screen during a high school chemistry lesson. The student can conduct the distillation experiment by touching the screen with his finger and by typing commands to the computer.

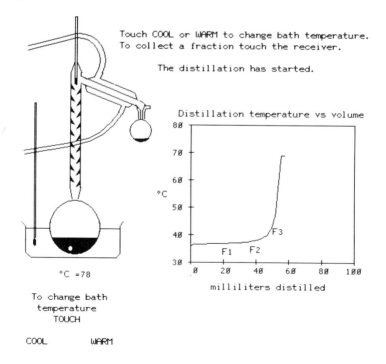

Touch COOL or WARM to change bath temperature.
To collect a fraction touch the receiver.

The distillation has started.

Distillation temperature vs volume

°C =78

To change bath
temperature
TOUCH

COOL   WARM

time are slow. And, if you make a mistake, you can erase an entire afternoon's work in an instant.

PLATO is different. When you tell PLATO to do something, you will have to wait, at most, an eighth of a second; and the computer offers you help when you run into trouble.

Also, PLATO acts like an electronic pony express. There are thousands of PLATO terminals scattered around the world. Friends at different schools and universities can send each other messages and play games long distance.

Control Data Corporation (CDC), PLATO's main sponsor, has the license to sell PLATO to schools around the world. Also, CDC is developing a system called MICRO-PLATO, which will run on small, classroom computers. The new system will have many of the features of PLATO and be inexpensive enough for schools to afford.

SMALLTALK IN THE CLASSROOM

For ten years Adele Goldberg worked with Alan Kay and the other scientists at Xerox to develop Smalltalk, a computer programming system of the future. Goldberg has been teaching Smalltalk to students in schools in Palo Alto, California, since 1974.

Goldberg dislikes classroom computers that drill students or teach them trivial facts and ideas. She wants her students to become expert designers and use Smalltalk as a master tool to design things that are important to them.

As Goldberg's students learn Smalltalk, they learn skills like how to represent and organize information, how to use their intuition to focus on what is important, how to devise rules to solve problems, how to make guesses, or hypotheses, and how to test those guesses to find the right answers to problems.

Adele Goldberg wants her students to use computers to design new "tools."

Goldberg's students use Smalltalk to build cartoon movies of drops of water falling and splashing in slow motion, and movies of horses galloping across the computer picture screen.

Students use Smalltalk to design new computer tools. For example, a student might build a special purpose calculator for converting Fahrenheit temperatures to Centigrade, or do an annual report for an imaginary corporation; or she might design a bridge, or develop a drafting tool (like a compass or protractor) for solving problems in three-dimensional geometry.

Using a Smalltalk simulation kit, a student might invent a new board game, or build a tiny cartoon on the picture screen that shows how a cookie factory makes cookies. The student might show how stoplights regulate heavy traffic in crowded city streets. He might compose and play a new song, with the musical notes appearing on the screen and the song coming out of the computer's speakers.

In all these examples, the student is developing new tools that other students can use, improve upon, or modify to meet their own needs.

29
BUILD YOUR OWN WORLD

WHEN YOU WALK into Seymour Papert's Learning Laboratory at MIT, the first thing you notice is that the teachers and young people are all sitting and lying around on the floor. The typical things found in a classroom—desks, pencils, and textbooks—are missing. Instead you see clear plastic boxes. On top of the boxes are buttons. Inside the boxes you see computer chips and wires. The boxes are connected by an electrical leash to little football helmets that scoot around the floor.

The plastic boxes are really tiny computers. The funny-looking helmets are robots.

The robots—known as *turtles*—have magic markers attached to their bellies. The students control the turtles by typing in orders on the computers. The students' commands make the turtles scurry around, drawing circles and squares on large sheets of paper taped to the floor. The students are delighted by the turtles' antics. Laughter and shouts of surprise fill the room.

Seymour Papert demonstrating a "micro world" he has created on the computer's picture screen.

For the last fifteen years, students have been programming turtles to draw pictures on the floor of Papert's learning lab. But the turtles are merely a starting point for other learning adventures. The students explore new ideas, rediscover scientific laws, and invent new worlds. On their way, they cover many advanced subjects that most schools consider too difficult except for the brightest students.

For example, many students who came into Papert's lab hating math left loving it. Problem students and young people with learning disabilities often became excellent turtle programmers and outperformed the other students in the class.

FASTEN YOUR SEATBELT!

When you sit down with a computer in your lap and the turtle on the floor in front of you, remember to put on your seatbelt. You are about to leave the world you know and travel to a turtle world.

A turtle world is an imaginary place inhabited by turtles. When you first arrive as a visitor to the turtle world, there are no rules or laws. You have to create everything from scratch by building the rules and laws into a turtle world program—a list of turtle commands.

You write the program on a piece of paper and then type the commands on the computer typewriter. The computer controls the turtle, and your program controls the computer.

To start your program, you type its name on the computer typewriter. The computer obeys each of your commands and sends orders to the little turtle robot. The robot moves through the imaginary turtle world obeying the laws you have set up.

You might draw a map of the world on the paper taped to your classroom floor. Your map might have rivers, bridges, roads, and mountains. You might add mazes, caves, and traps. Then you teach your turtle to move safely through the world you have invented. You teach it to find its way out of mazes, follow the roads, and avoid bottomless pits.

You can teach your turtle to become a mathematician and an artist. You can teach it to draw circles, triangles, spirals, and flowers on the floor. You can teach the turtle to draw its own world.

When you find teaching a "real" turtle on the floor too limiting, you can graduate to a light turtle on a computer TV. You can send your light turtle diving into an imaginary turtle world that you draw on the picture screen. It might be a world where all the laws of nature are topsy-turvy and upside down.

Greg Yob, a computer specialist, describes the thrill you can get from inventing a new turtle world:

. . . here is a tiny universe in which you can be God. Within the realms of expression that the computer can provide, you can build a world, define its laws, and watch the universe unfold. As your whim dictates, you can intervene at any time, and if you desire, the history of the universe can be changed and rewritten at will. Such a power this is!

Part VIII

THINKING
MACHINES
AND ROBOTS

30

SHAKEY, MARGIE, AND FRUMP

THE WORD ROBOT is modern, only sixty years old. It comes from the Czech word *robotnik*, which means worker or servant.

The word may be new, but we have been thinking and dreaming about robots ever since the dawn of time. Our history, legends, and myths are full of stories about creatures that look like us, think like us, and feel like us.

Until recently, our tools were too primitive to build machines that acted like living beings. Thinking robots could not be built from wood, heavy iron, clanking gears, or hissing steam engines.

Even if we had the proper tools, we still faced a mighty problem: Nobody knew how to build a robot.

INFORMATION MAKES THE WORLD RUN

To build a robot, we first needed to get some new ideas. This happened early in the twentieth century, when modern scientists came up with a new way of looking at the universe.

In the past, scientists had supposed that the universe ran solely on energy. Maybe it does run on energy, the modern scientists admitted. But it also runs on information.

Every event in the universe can be described in terms of information. In each event, information is transferred and exchanged. Information can explain why a cell divides and why magnets and electric circuits funnel and route electrons. Information can describe the way a person thinks and behaves.

We depend on information, just to stay alive. Our eyes, ears, and other senses are information-hungry. Every second our senses record huge gobs of information from the world around us, then send that information to our brain for its reaction.

THE EMPIRE STATE BUILDING COMPUTER

When the computer arrived, it fit the scientists' new ideas perfectly. Computers, like living creatures, are information machines.

Now the scientists had the right tool to build real robots. The scientists hoped that the robots' computer brains could perform the same functions as human brains—thinking, reasoning, understanding, remembering, and learning. The scientists hoped to turn the computers into thinking machines.

Unfortunately, the pioneers were so excited that they forgot two important facts. First, although early computers were faster than humans in solving problems of arithmetic and logic, they were crude and inexact copies of the human brain. An early computer had 20,000 memory and logic units (vacuum tubes), and could process from one to five thousand instructions a second.

The human brain, by contrast, is composed of 10,000 *billion* neurons. Each neuron is like a tiny computer. Together, the neurons can handle trillions of instructions at a time.

In the world of thinking machines, the computer was a pygmy, and the human brain a giant.

A comparison of early computers and the human brain went something like this. If you wanted to build a computer that was as powerful as the brain, you had to make the computer the size of the Empire State Building and power it with Niagara Falls.

But even if the computer were as complex and powerful as the human brain, how do we make it mimic the brain? In the 1940s and the 1950s, no one knew how the brain processed information. If the brain was a big mystery, how were we supposed to build a computer copy?

THE FIRST THINKING MACHINE

Eventually the pioneering scientists realized that they couldn't build a computer as powerful as the brain, and they couldn't program it to act like the brain. They were stuck.

That's when the real progress began. In the summer of 1956, the five fathers of the science of thinking machines got together on the campus of Dartmouth College, in Hanover, New Hampshire. The men were Claude Shannon, Marvin Minsky, John McCarthy, Allen Newell, and Herbert Simon. At that conference, McCarthy came up with a new term, *Artificial Intelligence* (or AI). AI was to be the science of turning computers into thinking machines and robots.

The five Dartmouth pioneers recognized that computers could not be built as exact replicas of the human brain. In fact, it didn't matter how the computers were built. All that mattered were results. A thinking machine had to learn to do things that would be considered intelligent if a human did them.

The key was to choose only one, narrow aspect of intelligence.

Allen Newell, Herbert Simon, and a programmer, Cliff Shaw, decided to create a computer program that could, on its own, solve logic problems. They called the program Logic Theorist (or LT, for short). The three pioneers packed into the program a large number of rules of mathematics and logic. Then, when they fed the program a theorem (a logical or mathematical statement), LT went ahead and proved it.

This may not seem like much. But it was something that, until December 1955, had never been done on a machine. Proving theorems is tough work for a math student and can even challenge a Ph.D. It is a job for a human, not a machine.

Yet the machine did it. Newell described LT as "kind of crude, but it works, boy, it works!"

LT was not just a computer parrot that echoed back answers given it by its human masters. Often, the proof the program came up with was completely different from the one Newell and Simon expected. Sometimes it was even better.

When a computer obeyed the instructions in LT, it became the world's first thinking machine.

SHAKEY'S TOY WORLD

Logic Theorist was a major breakthrough in trying to build a thinking machine out of a computer. But it was only the beginning. During the next twenty-five years, scientists invented all sorts of problem-solving programs. They also invented programs that could play chess and backgammon, programs that could translate Russian into English, and programs that could understand human speech.

They also invented robots.

The most famous robot was built in the late 1960s at SRI International (then known as the Stanford Research Institute). The robot's name was Shakey.

Shakey could move and see. He could understand commands given to him in English. He could only survive in a small, simple room, what some people called his toy world. But Shakey contributed a lot to scientists' understanding of how humans think, move, and see.

THE COMPUTER STORYTELLER

Scientists who build thinking machines don't spend their time dreaming up grand theories of intelligence. Instead, they pick one tiny part of intelligence and experiment.

Each time a scientist comes up with an idea, she immediately sits down and programs it into the computer. If the program runs as the scientist expected, good. But if the program doesn't work, the scientist doesn't give up. She sits down with the program and tries to figure out why it failed. Then she rewrites the program and tries again.

At Yale University, scientists have written programs that can answer questions, tell stories, and read newspaper accounts of world events. One program, FRUMP, can read and understand newspaper stories faster than a person can, and it remembers everything it reads. Gradually, FRUMP is gaining a common-sense understanding of our world.

One of the first programs developed at Yale was called MARGIE. MARGIE's job was to read sentences and try to figure out what they meant, regardless of how they were expressed. For example, MARGIE could figure out that two sentences, "John kissed Mary" and "Mary was kissed by John," meant the same thing.

MARGIE could demonstrate its understanding of a sentence by making inferences, or logical conclusions and observations, based on the original sentence. For example, if you typed in JOHN GAVE MARY AN ASPIRIN, MARGIE would read your sentence, analyze it, and make the following inferences:

> OUTPUT 1: JOHN BELIEVES THAT MARY WANTS AN ASPIRIN.
>
> OUTPUT 2: MARY IS SICK.
>
> OUTPUT 3: MARY WANTS TO FEEL BETTER.
>
> OUTPUT 4: MARY WILL EAT THE ASPIRIN.

For a machine to think so well is pretty amazing. But it is also clear that machines have a long way to go to catch up to us humans.

31
PUT YOUR DOCTOR ON A CHIP

AT STANFORD UNIVERSITY, a major Artificial Intelligence (AI) effort known as the Heuristic Programming Project was begun in 1965 and has operated continuously ever since. *Heuristic* means a rule-of-thumb, or intuitive, method of solving problems. We humans think this way all the time. But it is hard to teach to a computer.

Heuristic methods are important because they help a computer focus on the kind of knowledge it needs to solve a particular problem. This lets the computer zero in on a problem, just the way humans do. Without heuristics, the computer would take a different approach. It would search its entire memory for relevant information. Computer memories are incredibly huge. Even with a superfast computer, the search could take days or weeks or longer.

For example, people once thought computers could become world-class chess players because they were so fast. But, in the late 1940s, Claude Shannon built a chess-playing machine which he called Caissa, after the muse of chess. Shannon's experiments with Caissa, which did its thinking using electric circuits, showed him that building a foolproof chess-playing machine was virtually impossible.

Shannon explained that you could have the world's fastest, most powerful computer. You could program it to figure out all possible chess moves. If you had been able to start the program running at the dawn of the universe, today, billions of years later, it would still be grinding away trying to calculate all the moves in a single chess game.

The reason for this is that in a single game of chess, there are too many possible moves for even a super-computer to calculate.

But there is a way around this problem. The way is heuristics. People play good chess. People use heuristics—educated guesses—to judge a good move from a

Ed Feigenbaum mines knowledge locked in the heads of experts and then teaches it to a new generation of "smart" computers.

bad move, and to shorten the almost infinite amount of calculation they would have to do to figure out all chess moves.

High-speed supercomputers are being taught heuristics, and they are becoming good at chess and other games. They are so good, in fact, that they can beat most humans, even the experts.

Arcade computers, home computers, and tiny, hand-held computers are also learning how to play games. They can play chess, backgammon, Scrabble, tic-tac-toe, football, space war, and hundreds of other games. If you have ever played a computer, you know it can be a tough—and tricky—opponent.

MINING HUMAN BRAINS

Using heuristics and other ways to improve the judgment of computers, scientists at Stanford, under the direction of Edward Feigenbaum, Bruce G. Buchanan, and others, have developed computer programs to act as intelligent assistants to scientists, engineers, and doctors.

These programs come with names like DENDRAL, MYCIN, and MOLGEN. They discuss scientific experiments with human experts. The programs help the humans by providing the most up-to-date scientific findings, and by helping solve all sorts of knotty problems.

The programs have borrowed their problem-solving skills from some of the most brilliant human scientists in the world. According to Feigenbaum:

> . . . we are miners. We extract the gemstones of knowledge which are the private preserve of the expert practitioners in each field. . . .

> ... We are not creating robot geniuses, but
> rather making available knowledge and reason-
> ing skills, which up till now have been locked
> in the minds and judgments of a few experts.

The intelligent assistants and expert systems are constantly fed new facts and taught new reasoning and problem-solving skills so they can stay up to date. They are big, complex programs that run on high-speed computers tied into an international computer network. Any doctor, scientist, or engineer who has access to the network can talk over his current problems and projects with one of Feigenbaum's computer experts.

Doctors in remote areas of the world can use computer experts to help them diagnose their patients' illnesses. For example, when a doctor has a difficult case, or is confronted with a problem outside his specialty, he can plug a portable computer into a telephone and call one of the "computer doctors."

The programs are good at solving the types of problems people have the most trouble with. Over the years, hundreds of people have used these programs. They claim it's like having a top-notch expert working alongside them.

EXPERTS ON A CHIP

Will these computer experts ever appear in the home, so that you and I can use them?

Perhaps one day we might be able to buy a program that acts like a family doctor. It might be stored in a chip on our home computer. Whenever we felt sick, we could turn on our computer and activate the doctor chip. First we would tell it our symptoms. Then it would tell us what was making us feel bad.

Similarly, people could buy lawyer chips, minister chips, and psychiatrist chips to give them advice.

Will these chips ever become cheap enough for the average person to use on his home computer?

Feigenbaum admits they might be, but they aren't the same as the programs he and his colleagues have been developing. His experts and intelligent assistants are designed to be used by experts, not by the average person.

A scientist would have years of experience and a wealth of knowledge of his own to correctly interpret what the computer tells him. The average consumer wouldn't have this background, and he could easily be misled by the computer's advice. In fact, the computer might give him advice that could cause him injury or get him into trouble.

3 2

ROBOT PAINTERS AND GAME MACHINES

HAROLD COHEN IS a British-born artist who is a professor at the University of California at San Diego. In the mid-1960s, Cohen happened to meet Ed Feigenbaum. Feigenbaum convinced Cohen that there might be a way to teach computers how to become artists.

After talking to Feigenbaum, Cohen became a guest scholar at Stanford for two years. He read all the university library's materials on Artificial Intelligence (AI), the science of teaching machines how to think.

Cohen debated with the AI professors. He practically lived at the computer center, teaching himself how to write programs. He decided that he wanted to have a robot actually do his painting, so he designed and built the robot himself.

Next he decided that he needed a big computer to act as the robot's brain, so he persuaded a company to loan him a computer.

He spent months writing his robot's programs, then

Harold Cohen has taught his computer-controlled turtle robot to be an artist. On the wall is one of the turtle's original paintings.

months testing, correcting, and rewriting them. He wanted his robot to be a real artist, not just a doodler or a monkey playing with a paintbrush. He didn't want his robot to copy him. The robot had to be inventive and creative. Its art had to be fresh and unique.

Today, Cohen's intelligent robot has become a successful painter. It has had several exhibitions in prominent museums. Its paintings have been sold for large sums of money.

The robot—a "turtle"—receives instructions along a cable from the high-speed computer. It sees where it is on a huge canvas stretched on the floor by sending out ultrasonic beeps, just the way a bat does when it flies.

The beeps ricochet off two microphones on opposite corners of the canvas and return to the turtle. As soon as the beeps return, the turtle notifies the computer. The computer analyzes the time it takes the beeps to return and calculates the exact position of the turtle on the painting.

The turtle is not just Cohen's electronic puppet. Cohen has an elaborate theory of how he paints, what he finds beautiful, how people create images, and how they interpret them. He feeds these ideas and numerous rules of painting and drawing into the turtle. Then he turns it loose.

The turtle's art, like Cohen's, is playful, unrestrained, and colorful. The pictures the turtle paints are always a surprise to Cohen, since they are all new and original. The turtle never repeats itself.

THE COMPUTER GAME MASTER

Hans Berliner is a professor of computer science at Carnegie-Mellon University in Pittsburgh. Berliner is a specialist in thinking machines. He is also very good at teaching computers how to play games.

Berliner wrote a backgammon program that defeated the human world champion in Monte Carlo. Berliner admits that since backgammon is dependent on luck as well as skill, the next time the program and the ex-champ meet, the computer might lose and the person might win.

Hans Berliner is battling "Mighty-B," his world champion backgammon-playing program. When it is the computer's turn, a hand appears on the picture screen and moves the backgammon piece.

Backgammon is an easier game than chess. Thus far, no computer program has been able to defeat a world-class chess player. To encourage inventors to create smarter chess programs, Edward Fredkin, of MIT in Cambridge, Massachusetts, has offered a $100,000 prize to the creator of the first computer program to beat the world champion in chess.

Berliner says it will take programs a few years to get that good, but he fully expects a computer program to take the championship and grab the prize money by 1990, at the latest.

Berliner feels that we can build better game-playing programs by improving the programs' judgment. This is similar to the heuristic approach discussed earlier. A program with good judgment doesn't have to search its entire memory to find the knowledge it needs for its next move. It searches only through information that is relevant.

This is a risky, far-from-foolproof method. But it is what people do, and do rather well. As programs improve their judgment, they will become craftier and more clever. If Berliner is right, a clever, fast computer will soon prove the equal of the world chess champion.

You might think Berliner was a games' lover. Actually, he sees games as an arena in which he can perform experiments in Artificial Intelligence.

Berliner sees intelligence in an unusual way. Intelligence, Berliner says, is like sunshine hidden on the far side of a dirty, gunked-up window. According to Berliner:

> I want very badly to see the other side of that window. We all do. So every person scrapes away what he can. Games are my part of the window to scrape.

33

BUILD A ROBOT IN YOUR CLOSET

ROBOTS OF THE PAST were creatures of fantasy. They appeared in our myths, legends, books, and movies. But they were not real machines.

Today, for the first time in history, people are building real, working robots. The invention of the microcomputer has made this possible.

Chip-sized computers are powerful enough to act as a robot's brain, and control its movements, its limited senses, such as "hearing" and "seeing," and its ability to speak. These chips are also inexpensive.

As a result, robot kits are being offered for $400 to $2,000, and thousands of young people are building their own robots for only a couple of hundred dollars. These young inventors are building robot dogs with names like Rodney and Buster. They are building intelligent robot assistants, such as the Electronic Workman, Mike, and Reggie.

CHANGING A ROBOT'S "HABITS"

To be a robot a machine must be computer controlled and have mechanical and electrical sensors that act like human senses to receive information about the outside world.

The combination of sensors and a computer brain gives a robot the ability to act independently of any human control. It can learn by routing the information from its senses into its computer memory and by rewriting its own program.

Rewriting its own program?

Exactly. Intelligent robots can change the commands fed to them by their human masters and create new commands. They rewrite their programs as they receive new information from the outside world.

A robot's programs are like habits in a person. We form habits because they work. The way we eat, the way we get dressed, the way we look both ways crossing a busy road are all habits.

Habits keep working as long as the outside world remains the same. But as soon as the world changes, our habits have to change. This is what makes people so adaptable. We survive and are successful because we can adapt.

Programs in robots work only as long as the robot's world stays the same. When the world changes, the program should change. The best way to change the program is to let the robot change the program itself.

But programs don't always have to change.

If a robot's program anticipates changes in its world, the robot doesn't have to rewrite the program. It just has to accept information from its senses and then make a decision. It reacts to events in its environment. For example, if you moved a chair in front of a

Robot inventor Jonathan Kaplan is getting ready to place a microcomputer "brain" inside the chassis of his robot.

computer-controlled robot with ultrasonic eyes, the robot would see the chair and move around it.

CLASSROOM TURTLES AND ARTIFICIAL LIFE

The Terrapin Turtle (from Terrapin, Inc., of Cambridge, Massachusetts) is a popular, inexpensive robot. A little turtle robot is hooked to a small desktop computer via a cable leash. You can program the computer to control the turtle. Once you start the program by typing RUN, the turtle is completely under computer control.

Turtles are becoming very popular in classrooms. Students and teachers build them from kits, then program them to map rooms and explore mazes. In one school in North Carolina, two educators, Bruce Mitchell and his wife, Diane, are working with their students to construct an entire turtle city inhabited by robot turtles.

Young people are also building their own robots. Jonathan Kaplan is a young robot-building pioneer. Jonathan is fascinated with the idea of creating artificial life.

When Jonathan was very young, his mother went into his bedroom one day while Jonathan was at school. She began cleaning things up and found a dish of unpleasant-smelling stuff on the floor underneath Jonathan's dresser. She threw the ugly purple-and-green mixture away. That night when she asked Jonathan what it was, Jonathan exploded. "I was making life!" he cried. "And you ruined it!"

Jonathan and the other robot-builders also share a tremendous love of machines. Jonathan began building robots when he was only nine years old, after he saw a robot in a TV cartoon. His family lives in a New York City apartment, so Jonathan had to squeeze his robot laboratory into a walk-in closet in his bedroom.

Jonathan has built seven different robots, including ones that obey his spoken commands. Jonathan, like other computer pioneers, has gone on to other, related areas. His recent projects include work on a superfast computer using a fishnet of tiny brain chips, and work on intelligent computer robots that aid surgeons in performing difficult surgery.

34
ROBOTS AT WORK—FRIENDS OR FOES?

THIS COUNTRY HAS over ten thousand robots.

Most are at work in factories. They work on factory assembly lines. They spray-paint cars, weld car bodies, and assemble machine parts. They dip parts in molten furnaces, load products onto platforms, and inspect machines for missing parts and poor construction.

The U.S. used to be one of the most productive countries in the world. A flood of low-priced goods and services poured from our economy and spread across the world. But no longer. In recent years our economy has grown weak and less productive. Meanwhile, workers' wages have skyrocketed.

As a result, U.S. companies are turning to robots. Robots can help them compete with other countries in the world market. A robot can produce lots of new products at a low price.

A robot is expensive to buy, but it costs only $4.80 an hour to operate. In contrast, a blue-collar worker gets paid from $15 to $20 an hour.

Also, a robot can do the same job over and over again, hundreds of times, without making a mistake. It never gets tired, or bored, or takes a coffee break. Robots never get sick, they don't get depressed, and they never show up at the factory with a hangover. They can handle jobs that are tedious, bulky, and dangerous. If there's an accident, the robot ends up injured or with squashed fingers, not a person.

What do worker robots look like?

They do not look like the robots you've seen in comic books and movies. They look more like huge gorilla arms perched on top of fire plugs. When the arms move, they make strange noises.

Industrial robots look like a cannon with a hand mounted on the end of the barrel. The robots can weld, paint, and lift heavy crates and machine parts. Robots are well-suited for factory jobs that are dull, dirty, or dangerous.

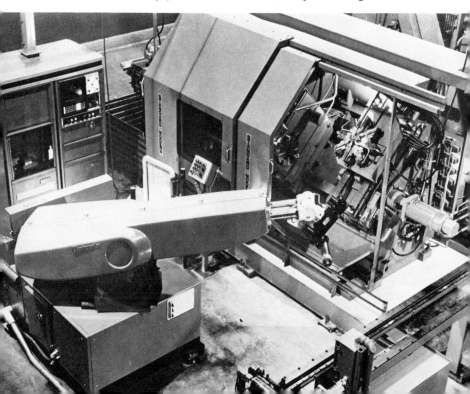

Joseph Engelberger has been building industrial robots for more than twenty years.

Most worker robots of the past were not equipped with sensors, devices that enable them to get information from the outside world. Modern robots, however, are being produced with a limited ability to see, hear, and touch.

Programs that control the robots are getting much more intelligent. Smart robots are now appearing in laboratories and factories. These robots have a limited awareness of themselves, their work, and the world around them. Many robots now work alongside human workers on conveyor lines.

Who are the robots' creators? Joseph Engelberger, for one. Engelberger is the president of Unimation Inc., in Danbury, Connecticut. He is known as the "father of industrial robots." His company, Unimation, started producing robots over twenty years ago.

Joseph Engelberger believes that robots will help our economy. But he feels their impact will be gradual and spread over a period of decades. Engelberger says that he is a firm believer in the technological fix. By this he means that he thinks technology, such as robots, can solve many of our economic and social problems.

According to Engelberger, robots help us produce things faster and cheaper. Increased productivity means a growth in national wealth. Increased national wealth means more money in all our pockets.

Robots may bring great benefits. But what happens if too many robots are produced all at once? "They steal people's jobs," says Harley Shaiken. Shaiken is a consultant to the United Auto Workers in Detroit. He disagrees with Engelberger that robots are being introduced gradually.

Shaiken wrote an article for the *New York Times* entitled "A Robot Is after Your Job." In the article he claims that there is tremendous pressure on American industry to replace human workers with robots.

As a result, he feels that our economy will be rapidly "robotized" over the next ten years. Each robot that a factory uses can continue working year after year. Also, each robot can work three eight-hour shifts at high speed. This means an average robot can replace several human workers. Since robot turnover will be almost nonexistent, new robots won't replace older robots— they'll replace humans.

Shaiken claims that he is not against the introduction of robots. He agrees that the U.S. must increase its productivity to remain competitive with Western European countries and Japan. But he wants workers who lose their jobs to robots to be retrained and offered a new job.

A ROBOT WITH EYES ON ITS WRIST

James Albus is the head of the robotics laboratory at the National Bureau of Standards in Gaithersburg, Maryland. Albus has built a robot arm with a TV camera on its wrist. Albus's robot uses its "eyes" to assemble a

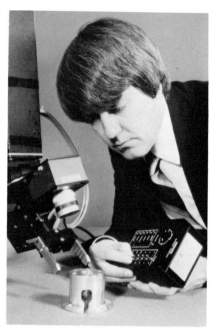

Jim Albus is teaching his robot to pick up a machine part. The robot's "eye" is a camera mounted on its wrist.

machine from many machine parts strewn around a table.

Albus has spent years designing and thinking about robots. He believes that the world is on the brink of a new industrial revolution. He feels that robots will completely change our lives.

Albus envisions factories and industries that employ no human workers, only robots.

Eventually robots will take over jobs in all parts of our economy. We will see robot office workers, robot clerks, robot salesmen, robot bankers, and robot doctors.

If robots do all the work, what should we pay people? Do we pay everybody the same?

We may decide to pay some people more. But how much more? And why do they deserve to make more than other people?

Joseph Engelberger agrees with Albus's predictions. Robots are going to change everything.

Engelberger also believes, as do the Japanese, that all unskilled workers will be replaced by robots. He feels that, in the long-term future, the only secure jobs will require extensive training. The Japanese call the type of people who will fill these jobs *knowledge workers*.

According to an important government official, the Japanese are rebuilding their economy to prepare for the arrival of smart computers and working robots. By the middle of the twenty-first century, Japanese experts feel there will only be three classes of workers in Japan: knowledge workers, computers, and robots.

Part IX

CREATIVE COMPUTERS AND COMPUTER GENIUS

35
TEACHING A COMPUTER TO SEE

DAVID AHL BELIEVES we can teach computers to do things that are creative. He believes computers can be fun.

Creative computing is common now. But it wasn't twenty-five years ago when Dave saw his first computer. Back then, most people saw computers as giant calculators. Computers weren't supposed to be fun. They were for serious business.

But Dave felt that computing could be fun when he first learned to program, as a student at Cornell University in 1956. A week after learning to program Cornell's old vacuum-tube computer, Dave invented his first computer game. He's been inventing games ever since.

Over the next twenty years, Dave created a lot of new games and shared them with people all over the country. He translated the games into dozens of different computer languages and got them running on many different kinds of computers.

Late in 1974, Dave recognized that a huge group of

Many years ago, Dave Ahl saw that computers could be far more than dull bookkeeping machines and scientific number-crunchers. He saw that computers could be used creatively—for learning and for fun.

people were interested in having fun with computers and in programming computers creatively. Perhaps a new magazine could tie these people together and tell them about the latest computer products and games.

Dave retreated to his home office, and after some nonstop typing, he came up with a sixty-eight-page computer newspaper he called *Creative Computing*. Dave tracked down the names and addresses of everyone he knew in computers. Then he got his kids together, and everybody hand-addressed the newspaper for mailing.

The Ahl family drove the copies of the newspaper to the post office and sent them off in the mail.

Would the newspaper fly?

Within weeks Dave had his answer: Yes. The response was overwhelming. Hundreds of people thought as Dave did: Computers weren't just number crunchers and electronic paper-pushers. They were fun, too. There was a huge market for creative computing.

THE PAPER CLOUDBURST

We are being flooded by a cloudburst of paper.

Much of it comes from computers. Computer printers spit out over 240 billion pages each year. The number is growing so rapidly that the *extra* paper produced by computers each year would equal a stack of telephone directories several thousand miles high.

People are overwhelmed by the millions of facts and figures that computers spray at them. There is no way to absorb so many numbers and words. So people stop trying.

It's like when you take a shower. Can you imagine trying to swallow all the water as it sprays out of the shower head? It would be impossible. Instead, you let the water bounce off your head and wash over your body.

The same goes for information. People just let it wash over them. Better to ignore it rather than try to drink it all in.

A PICTURE IS WORTH A BILLION NUMBERS

Unfortunately, there is a lot of useful information buried in the cloudburst of paper. But how do we get at this information?

One way is to teach computers to weed out all the irrelevant information and save only what we need. Intelligent programs, similar to the FRUMP program at Yale, or the DENDRAL program at Stanford, might screen the news for us and select only those subjects we want to learn more about.

But how can we digest all the numbers the computer produces?

One way is to turn those numbers into pictures. The pictures are known as *computer graphics*.

3-D SURFACE GRAPH
"The Volcano"

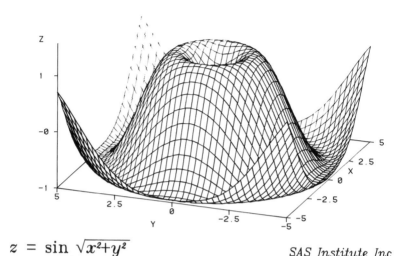

$$z = \sin \sqrt{x^2+y^2}$$

SAS Institute Inc

A computer can turn a complicated equation into a three-dimensional picture of a volcano.

Someone once said that a picture is worth a thousand words. Today, a beautiful, clear, computer-produced picture might take the place of millions of confusing computer-produced numbers.

The picture might be a map of the U.S., with mountains representing the distribution of population around the country. It might be a chart showing how the average person spends his or her income. A pizza could represent the person's income. Major expenses could be represented as slices of the pie.

The computer picture might be a color drawing of a person's lung or a satellite map of the Midwest showing patches of diseased wheat. Or it might be a moving picture of an approaching runway to help teach a new pilot how to land an airplane.

The pilot doesn't even have to leave the ground. The

Scientists once had to visualize complex molecules from long strings of numbers. Now a computer can turn the numbers into a colorful molecule "movie."

The inside of a computerized flight simulator looks like the cockpit of a large airplane. The plane's windows are really computer picture screens. As the student pilot steers the simulator, the computer creates the view he would see if he were flying a real plane.

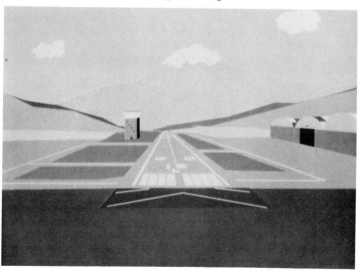

If you look out the "window" of this flight simulator, you see a formation of F16 fighter planes streaking through the sky. Your F16 is a member of that formation.

picture is part of a machine that looks like the cockpit of a real plane. The cockpit rolls and weaves, just like in a real plane. But the windows aren't real. They are computer picture screens, hooked into the cockpit controls.

Computer-controlled machines are used to teach soldiers, pilots, drivers, divers, sea captains and astronauts. They are called *simulators* because they simulate, or mimic, a real vehicle, like an airplane or a spaceship.

Simulators are becoming very advanced and realistic. At the National Maritime Research Center in Kings Point, New York, there is a simulator with a large computer picture screen window that gives you a 240-degree view. That's a picture as wide as you can see by twisting your head to the left as far as it will go, then swinging it to the right as far as it will go.

The simulator makes you feel as if you are on the bridge of a big ship entering New York Harbor.

Through the computer-screen window, you see the harbor and the New York City skyline.

In the harbor, numerous ships come and go all around you. You guide your own ship by operating the simulator's controls. As you turn the ship, the picture on the simulator screen changes, just as if you were piloting a real freighter.

Your ship is completely under your control. As captain, you try to maneuver around the other ships. However, if you aren't careful, you could smash into a ship like a battering ram. Or you might crash, head-on, into one of New York's giant bridges.

THE WORLD THROUGH THE EYE
OF THE COMPUTER

Today dozens of companies manufacture computer *graphics terminals*—computer keyboards with TV screens.

Scientists taught a computer what mountains look like; then the computer drew this picture of an imaginary mountain.

Almost all personal computers are built so you can plug them into your TV and make pictures. Depending on the type of computer or terminal, it might make simple black-and-white stick figures, or it might paint realistic pictures in full color.

Some computer pictures are so realistic, they look like photographs.

Lauren Carpenter is a computer scientist who specializes in teaching computers to draw realistic pictures. Lauren recently taught his computer to draw a picture of a mountain range. The computer's picture looks exactly like a photo taken by a hardy mountaineer, thousands of feet up the sheer face of a snow-covered mountain.

Amazingly, the picture is completely artificial. The mountains in the picture were drawn by a computer program that was trained to understand what real

Artist Paul Xander used a computer to create this picture. The title of the picture is "Sierra."

mountains look like. The program created some artificial mountains out of millions of numbers and hundreds of rules, then painted the mountains on the computer's picture screen.

If you didn't like the computer's mountains, you could erase the screen. A few seconds later, a new mountain range would appear, compliments of the computer's imagination.

Computer screens haven't always been able to make pictures. In the 1940s and early 1950s, people used computer screens as part of the computer's memory. Later, in the mid-'50s, people used picture screens as "electronic paper." For example, when a programmer typed in commands or information on the computer typewriter, a copy would appear on the picture screen.

No one knew how to make pictures on a computer screen, just numbers and words. Everyone knew computers were good at arithmetic, but no one realized that computers could translate numbers into pictures.

Then along came Ivan Sutherland.

THE ROBOT AND THE TRANSISTOR

Ivan Sutherland grew up in Pittsburgh in the 1950s. Ivan and his brother were fascinated by computers and robots. They even built a battery-powered, light-sensing robot that had bumpers and could find its way through a complicated maze.

The boys corresponded with Gray Walters and Claude Shannon who had invented maze-conquering robot mice. They once even took their robot all the way to Bell Laboratories in Murray Hill, New Jersey, so they could show it off to Shannon, who was their idol.

By corresponding with Bell Labs scientists, young Ivan learned about a new device called a transistor. A

Ivan Sutherland in 1973. Ivan's "Sketchpad" system showed the world that computers could draw and paint pictures.

transistor looked like a Tootsie Roll with three wires sticking out. It could route pulses of electricity through a robot or a computer. It was supposed to be the key to miniature, superfast computers of the future.

Ivan desperately wanted a transistor of his own. After weeks of saving his allowance, he took his money down to an electronics store and, for fifteen dollars, purchased a single transistor.

Ivan was so excited about owning a transistor, that he carried it everywhere. His mother was afraid that he would lose it, so she put it in her jewelry box for safekeeping.

Ivan graduated from high school, went to Carnegie-Mellon University, in Pittsburgh, and earned his B.S. in Electrical Engineering. He got married, and he and his wife, Marcia, moved to Pasadena, California, so Ivan could get his Master's Degree at the California Institute of Technology.

While at Caltech, Ivan received a visit from Marvin Minsky and Oliver Selfridge, two famous computer scientists from MIT in Cambridge, Massachusetts. The two scientists, anxious to have Ivan transfer his work to MIT, described in glowing terms a new computer they had at MIT's Lincoln Laboratories. They offered Ivan a summer job working with the computer, known as the TX-O.

Ivan was excited by the idea of working with a fancy new computer. He finished his Master's Degree at Caltech in only nine months. At the end of the term, he and Marcia headed to Cambridge. As soon as the two arrived in town, Ivan rushed over to see the TX-O.

After his first visit with the TX-O, Ivan returned home and told Marcia, "Boy! They really have computing at MIT!"

Ivan was thrilled. He could operate the TX-O directly, using a computer typewriter and picture screen. He didn't have to type his instructions on cards or paper tape and then wait for hours to catch the computer's attention. He could sit down at the terminal and type commands to the computer. It would immediately talk back.

With the TX-O around, Minsky and Selfridge had no trouble keeping Ivan happy at MIT. That fall, he entered the Ph.D. program in Computer Science.

Ivan hoped to continue working with the TX-O, but he was disappointed. The demand for the computer increased drastically during the school year, and Ivan was, after all, just a lowly graduate student. He never got a chance to use the computer.

But he didn't give up.

The computer was in use all during the day, but it was free every night after midnight. So Ivan, Marcia, and their two kids, set up a new schedule for Ivan to follow. At 3:30 every morning, Marcia would get Ivan up, feed him breakfast, and send him off to the computer lab. She'd go back to bed until seven or eight, then get up with the kids.

Ivan, meanwhile, would rush over to the lab, sit

down at the terminal, and have the computer all to himself until the first professors and computer operators arrived.

THE FIRST ELECTRONIC SKETCHPAD

During one early-morning session with the computer, Ivan was playing with the picture screen. He had seen people type dashes on the screen. But no one, he realized, had ever programmed the computer to draw.

Ivan wanted to write a program that would cause the computer to draw a simple line on the picture screen. To do this he had to face several problems no one else had ever faced.

These are some of the questions Ivan asked himself: How do I describe a line to the computer? What instructions will make the computer actually draw the line? How do I tell the computer where to start the line and where to stop it? Should the line be of a fixed size, like a pole, or should it be elastic, like a rubber band?

Over the next two and a half years, Ivan worked on this problem. Finally, he figured out how to make the computer draw a line. Then he figured out a way to make the computer draw a square, and then a triangle. One day, he practically danced around the laboratory. He had made the computer draw a circle!

But Ivan didn't stop there. He taught the computer to draw beautiful 3-D shapes like spheres, cones, and cubes. He taught the computer to spin the shapes round and round. He taught the computer to shrink the shapes and enlarge them.

Step by step, Ivan blazed a trail into the world of computer graphics. After two and a half years, he proudly unveiled Sketchpad, a complete computer picture-making program.

David Evans pioneered "continuous-tone" computer pictures that look like photographs of real objects.

Ivan's enthusiasm about making pictures was contagious. According to Marcia, "Wherever Ivan was, people showed up and got excited. When Ivan was around, things just started happening."

WHAT GOOD ARE COMPUTER PICTURES?

In the late 1960s, Ivan joined another computer graphics pioneer, David Evans, and set up a computer graphics company, Evans and Sutherland Corporation.

By 1968, Ivan and David had moved the company to Salt Lake City, Utah, and had produced their first two-color picture-making computers.

The computers made beautiful pictures, but, mysteriously, no one wanted to buy them. According to Marcia, "Just because you build a better mousetrap doesn't mean the world is going to beat a path to your door. First, it seems, you have to teach the world why it's important to trap mice."

The problem was no one knew about computer pic-

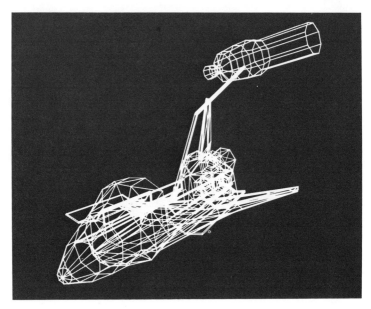

A wire-frame diagram of the Space Shuttle unloading a satellite into orbit around the earth.

tures, or what they were good for. When Ivan and David talked to prospective customers, they'd respond, "Computers produce numbers, not pictures. Why would anyone want pictures?"

But David and Ivan didn't give up. They explained how colorful pictures could take the place of hundreds of pages of paper, and millions of numbers. Picture-making computers could be used, for example, as the windows of flight simulators to train pilots to fly jets.

David and Ivan eventually won their battle. People finally recognized the importance of computer pictures.

Eventually, dozens of companies were building picture-making computers. Ivan and David were the founders of what is today a multibillion-dollar industry.

36
THE ALPHABET ARTIST

DONALD KNUTH IS a musician. His favorite instrument is the pipe organ. His pipe organ is in his home. Since he couldn't find an organ he liked, he made his own. He built it in his spare time.

Some people say that musicians make the best programmers. If there ever was a brilliant programmer, it is Donald Knuth.

Don is a mathematician and professor of Computer Science at Stanford University. He is the author of the most famous set of textbooks about computers.

A few years ago, Don was working on a new, revised edition of his textbooks. The first edition appeared many years ago and had been printed by an old-fashioned method used on almost all high-quality books at the time.

While Don was preparing for his books' second edition, publishers were switching to a new technique in which computers create letters photographically. But Don thought the new technique would make his books "look terrible." As in the case of his organ, since he couldn't find the kind of product he wanted, he decided to build what he needed.

Don was supposed to take a year's leave from his teaching job at Stanford and go to South America. But he canceled his trip and headed for the rare books collection at the Stanford University Library.

Don began his research into book publishing with Johann Gutenberg, the German genius who invented the modern method of printing.

Each element of Gutenberg's type was a piece of metal with a raised letter, number, or symbol of punctuation. When the metal was dipped in ink and pressed against paper, it left the image of the character on the paper.

Originally, each piece of metal was fashioned by hand. To print a book or newspaper, each letter or number had to be arranged by hand. Later, machines were built to melt and refashion the metal for each new book or newspaper. The process was still mechanical and quite slow.

Most recently, the letters and numbers have been reproduced photographically. This is faster, but the quality of the book or newspaper suffers, since the letters and numbers are fuzzier than those produced by the printer's ink and metal type.

CHANGING NUMBERS INTO LETTERS

Don was upset that newer books were nowhere as well done as older books produced on old-fashioned printing presses. These presses were rapidly disappearing. Yet Don wanted his new books printed cheaply and beautifully. Perhaps he could teach a computer how to do it.

As a mathematician, Don realized that letters in the alphabet are shapes: circles, squares, and triangles. Any shape can be expressed as a mathematical formula. Since letters are shapes, they must have a for-

Donald Knuth playing an organ that he built himself. Knuth thinks programming a computer can be as artful as composing and playing beautiful music.

mula, too. Like a detective, Don began tracking down the formula for each letter in the alphabet.

Don was successful. He found formulas for all the letters.

Don fed the formulas into the memory of his computer. Then he taught the computer to transform the formulas into letters. Last he taught the computer to draw the letters on a picture screen.

By punching a couple of buttons, Don could make the computer mold the letters like clay. He could make the letters taller, shorter, fatter, or skinnier. He could make them lean over, lie down, or stand on their heads. He could do all this in just a couple of minutes.

Fascinated, Don set out to develop a computer language that would enable an average person to design

3.1415926535897...

**The decimal fraction of the number "pi" (3.14159 . . .)
never ends. Don Knuth's Metafont program shows pi's infinitely long string of numbers getting smaller as the fraction gets smaller.**

letters at a computer typewriter and TV screen, and then press a button and have a computer print them out. Don called this language Metafont.

Similarly, he worked on another language that would let a person tell the computer how he wanted his words grouped on a page and how the pages should be grouped into chapters of a book, or sections of a paper or article. This language Don called TEX.

Don could make a fortune by guarding the secret of his invention and forming a company to sell it to the world. Instead, he is publishing all the details of his two languages, and he is helping companies install them on their computers. People will soon be able to use small, desktop computers to design their own letters and print their own books.

Don says that he wants to share his new system with other people, but, he says, "the real reason I give it away for free is, I'm not doing this for work, I'm doing it for fun."

Knuth told his Metafont program to print the word "mathematics" over and over, each time increasing the randomness of the computer's pen positions.

mathematics
mathematics
mathematics
mathematics
mathematics
mathematics
mathematics
mathematics
mathematics
mathematics
mathematics
mathematics

37
THE ELECTRONIC BOOK

IT IS SOMETIME in the future.

Imagine that you are in your bedroom studying for an exam.

You have your history text in front of you. You are trying to memorize the names of the presidents of the United States.

You get as far as Andrew Jackson, the seventh president. Then your eyelids droop shut. You stayed up most of last night to see a horror movie on the Late Show, and you are dead tired.

Out of nowhere a voice says, "Name the seventh president of the United States."

You open your eyes. "Huh?" you say.

"Name the seventh president of the United States," repeats the voice.

You look down at your history text. The words on the page have all disappeared. In their place is a picture of a stern-looking man in a soldier's uniform. Under the picture are the words "Seventh President of the U.S."

You know who it is. "Andrew Jackson," you say.

"Right," says the voice. The voice is coming from your textbook. Your textbook is talking.

The textbook flashes a new picture. It's a man with fuzzy sideburns and a funny-looking tie. He looks like he's trying hard not to sneeze. Under his picture are the words "Eighth President of the U.S."

"Name the eighth president of the United States," your textbook says.

This is a tough question. You try hard to remember. "Was it Henry Polk?" you ask.

"Wrong," says the textbook. "Polk was the eleventh president. And his first name was James. Try again."

"Van Buren," you mumble. "Was it Martin Van Buren?"

"Correct. Good thinking," says the textbook. "Now name . . ."

THE BOOK OF THE FUTURE

The scene above seems right out of science fiction. After all, books can't talk to you and flash pictures and words like a slide show or movie. At least books made of paper can't.

Yet, within ten years, a new kind of book will appear. It will talk, listen, and flash colorful, moving pictures. It will be made of metal and plastic, instead of paper. It will come in the form of a *book player*, just like a cassette recorder. It will "play" words, pictures, and ideas, instead of music.

A tiny computer chip will store all the book's words. The chip will be packaged in a protective plastic cartridge. To begin "reading" your book, you'll plug the cartridge into your book player and press the ON button.

Instead of pages there will be a small, flat TV screen.

The book's words will flash on the screen one page at a time. When you press the ON button, the first page will appear on the screen. When you are finished reading a page, you will push the NEXT PAGE button and a new page will instantly appear.

But what if you are tired of reading? Or what if you are busy working and can't hold the book or look at its pages? Then you can press the AUTO READ button and close your eyes. You just have to listen.

The book won't show only letters and words. It will also flash pictures. School textbooks will come with oral quizzes, questions, and exercises built right in. You'll have to stay alert. Just when you start to fall asleep, the electronic textbook may fire a tough question at you.

FROM PAPER TO ELECTRONICS

Pocket-sized electronic books are still in the future. But they are the dream of Andy Van Dam, a brilliant computer pioneer.

Andy is chairman of the Department of Computer Science at Brown University, in Providence, Rhode Island. For the last ten years, he, his students, and other professors have been trying to turn books of paper into books made of metal, glass, and wires.

Andy has already developed an experimental book. You read Andy's book by asking a computer program to display the book's pages on a beautiful color picture screen.

Some people want to know why Andy is trying to kill the book. Andy says he isn't trying to kill the book. He admits he likes books, especially fine old books made out of good paper and bound in leather. But, he says, this type of book is very rare. Today's books are

Andy van Dam is creating a "dragon" picture that will appear in his Electronic Book.

made out of cheap materials, and they quickly deteriorate.

Andy wants to see books evolve and keep up with the latest technology. In his Electronic Book, Andy would like to keep all the virtues of today's books. For example, books are small and can be carried anywhere. They don't have to be plugged in or frozen before they can be read. They are pretty sturdy and rarely break.

Books are easy to use—anytime, anywhere. When you need information from a book, you can refer to the table of contents or index. Also, when you read a book, you read it privately and at your own pace. Reading a book is a personal, unique experience that may shape your whole life.

However, books made of paper are getting more and more expensive. In our fast-paced world, too, when a book reaches the reader, it may already be obsolete and out of date.

Furthermore, books are also having a hard time competing with electronic media such as radio and especially TV. A book uses an artificial format to communicate—the printed word. Television, on the other hand, talks to you. It has colorful, moving pictures with characters, action, and adventure.

Andy feels that in another ten years, an economic

crunch will force book publishers to begin producing electronic books and printing fewer paper books. He is trying to make his electronic book have all the good features of paper books and also some of the attractive features of television. His "book" will be portable, private, and easy to use. It will display a page at a time on the screen, but if you want to move around in the book, you will just point to one of the tiny "pages" in the margins, and the computer will put that page on the screen instead.

Andy's electronic book was inspired by Vannevar Bush's imaginary memex computer. (See Chapter 21) Andy's book resembles memex. For example, as you are reading the book, you can personalize it by making comments, notes, and even drawings in the book (on the picture screen).

Also, you can build a trail as you read the book, or as you read several books. This trail is like the memex trail. As you go hopping and skipping from book to book, the computer keeps track of your trail. When you are all done, the computer remembers every step. Later, when you want to follow the trail, you can get the computer to give you an instant replay.

Andy's book won't be quiet and sit on a table. It will be active. It will have artificial intelligence, it will be a thinking machine. It will talk to you, answer your questions, and help you get the information you need. It will have animated color pictures. It may even play music.

BOOKS THAT CHANGE AND GROW

With all these features, it's easy to see books in a whole new light. For example, the book of the future can still be portable and reliable. But it will also be something that you can change.

Right now, imagine that you grabbed a red pen and wrote in this book. What would happen?

It would be okay if the book is yours. But what if you borrowed the book from your library? What would your librarian say if you returned the book with lots of jokes and witty remarks scribbled in the margins?

She would probably tell your mom and dad and then fine you for defacing the book.

Andy's electronic book will be different. It will be a small black cartridge. Inside the cartridge will be several computer memory chips. Some of the chips will store the original book; the other chips will be empty. They will be like endless margins and blank pages for you to add ideas of your own.

As you read the book, it may ask you questions or invite you to write down your thoughts and feelings. The book might give you lots of good ideas or make you remember something from another book, or something that once happened to you. You might agree with one part of the book, then get angry and disagree with another part. You can add anything you want to the book. You can personalize it by making notes and adding your own thoughts, ideas, and remarks.

When you return your electronic book to the library, your ideas will be stored in the memory chips. Then the next person who checks out the book can read just the original book or also read your ideas.

38

THE COMPUTER GOES TO HOLLYWOOD

HAVE YOU EVER seen Walt Disney's *Pinocchio*? Remember when the giant whale Monstro swallowed Pinocchio and held him prisoner in a belly as big as a cathedral?

Or *Fantasia*? Remember the terrible battle between two huge dinosaurs—a Stegosaurus and a Tyrannosaurus Rex? Remember the evil creatures who came alive at night on Bald Mountain? Remember poor Mickey Mouse and the dancing broomsticks which tried to drown him in buckets of water?

Did you see *One Hundred and One Dalmatians*? Remember Cruella de Vil? She was the demonic woman who kidnapped the dalmatian puppies so she could skin them for a fur coat. Think about the chase scene down the mountain, with Cruella's car spitting fire, and Cruella herself looking like an angry fiend from hell.

These were Disney masterpieces. They were full-length animated features, king-sized cartoons. Every character was drawn by hand. Each scene was drawn by hand. Dozens of artists teamed up and worked thousands of hours to produce all the still paintings that, when shown together very quickly, made the cartoon characters come alive.

The pictures were incredibly realistic. The heroes were brave. The villains were frightening and evil. Action filled the screen from start to finish.

The pictures used to roll out of the studios, year after year. Then, in the 1960s, the studios' flood of new animations dried to a trickle. All that's left are the reruns.

Why?

Because full-length, animated cartoons had become tremendously expensive.

THE END OF THE GOLDEN AGE

In order to produce a quality animated film, you need to have artists draw hundreds of thousands of individual, full-color pictures. Each picture might only be slightly different, but it has to be completely drawn and colored.

Walt Disney Studios pioneered full-color, high-quality animated films. The 1930s, '40s, and '50s were the Golden Age of Cartoons. Disney had hundreds of animators working, turning out such classics as *Sleeping Beauty*, *Dumbo*, and *Snow White*.

Even though these movies were a great success, costs rose so fast that, after a while, it became unprofitable to do animated films with any level of detail, craftsmanship, or quality. Almost the only type of animations that remained by the late '60s and '70s were "quick-and-dirty" animations used for Saturday morning cartoon shows.

The cheaper animations used several shortcuts that significantly decreased their quality. For example, dozens of pictures in a row would be exactly the same, except that the characters' lips moved. Different chase scenes might be repeated several times. The action of the characters might be jerky and ragged because the animators didn't make frames to capture each fine detail of the characters' movements. The background in the animation might be blank, or hastily drawn in, or repetitive.

COMPUTER CARTOONS

In the mid-1980s, animation has again become popular, thanks to the computer. The computer does not produce films automatically. Human artists still do the original artwork.

The computer helps the artist in two major ways. First, the computer helps him or her work faster. Second, it frees the artist from performing many boring, tedious chores, such as filling in colors and painting the same, exact scene forty times in a row.

An artist can draw an original picture—with scenery and characters—using a special pen plugged into the computer. As he or she draws, the same picture appears on the computer's TV screen and in the computer's memory.

When a picture is drawn, the artist can choose colors for the characters and scenery by touching a "menu" of colors shown on the screen. Then the artist can touch the area in the picture that is to be painted that color. The computer colors the area automatically.

For example, let's say the artist has just drawn a robot and wants to make it metallic blue. She touches the blue color on the menu and then the robot. Instantly, the computer paints the robot blue.

Let's say the robot is crouching with a light saber in its right hand. The scene calls for the robot to leap onto a tall ledge, while holding the saber. In the past, a good animation film would have required the artist to draw dozens of "in-betweener" pictures that showed the robot in a crouch, flying through the air, and ending up on the ledge. This would have made the robot's jump look natural, lifelike, and realistic. Now the artist has to draw only two pictures: the robot in the crouch and the robot on the ledge. Then the computer automatically draws and colors in all the in-between pictures.

STAR WARS AND TRON

Ed Catmull is a wizard at using computers to create special effects for movies. Recently Ed was hired by Lucasfilm to produce the computerized special effects for future episodes of the Star Wars saga.

Ed spent his first year at Lucasfilm getting ready. He built several high-speed animation computers. He designed revolutionary new special effects. He hired the top artists and computer experts in the world.

Now Ed has begun teaching the computers to create animated pictures that will come in all colors and in three dimensions. The pictures will be inserted in the midst of live action in upcoming Star Wars movies.

Dick Lundin, an artist, used a computer to paint this picture of a "Panzer" robot. The picture is a frame from "The Works," a full-length, animated computer movie.

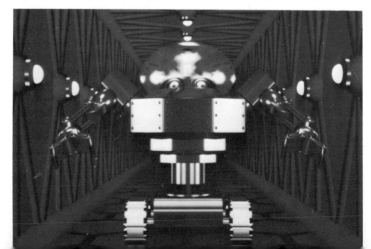

Artist Paul Zander used a computer to paint this picture of a castle on a mountaintop. The picture is a frame from "Puss 'N Boots," an animated computer movie.

They will be so exciting and lifelike that you'll think they are real.

Walt Disney Productions is also making use of the new special effects computers. For example, computers played a major role in the new Disney movie *TRON*. *TRON* is about Flynn, a video game genius who gets kidnapped to the world inside the computer. MCP, an evil computer program, captures Flynn and transports him to a bizarre game grid, where he becomes an electronic gladiator and must constantly fight battles just to stay alive.

To produce the incredible scenes in *TRON*, Disney hired some of the most famous computer animation companies in the world. These companies taught their computers to create some of the amazing special effects.

39

A WINDOW INTO THE FOURTH DIMENSION

WE CAN TEACH computers to make beautiful pictures. These pictures might train us to pilot a ship into New York harbor. They might illustrate an electronic book or be the scenes and characters in an animated movie.

For Ivan Sutherland, the computer screen was a fascinating window into the computer. But it can also become a window into the mysterious fourth dimension.

What is the fourth dimension? First, let's start with dimensions one, two, and three.

The first dimension is length. A line is of the first dimension. It has length, but nothing more.

The second dimension is width. A square is of the first and second dimensions. It has length and width, but is flat.

The third dimension is height. We are creatures of the first, second, and third dimensions. We have length, width, and height.

The world around us seems to have only three di-

242

Artist Duane Palyka uses a computer light pen to paint a self-portrait.

mensions. Trees, clouds, and trolleycars all have only three dimensions.

So what is the fourth dimension? Is it the home of ghosts and demons?

Ancient philosophers, such as Aristotle and Ptolemy, were convinced that a fourth dimension was impossible. Later, in the 1600s, the English mathematician John Wallis wrote that the fourth dimension was a "Monster in Nature."

But, early in the twentieth century, Albert Einstein discovered a real fourth dimension. The fourth dimension is time. The three dimensions hurtle through time like a planet falling through space. Einstein created many scientific theories based on the fourth dimension.

We can feel time passing, but we cannot see it the way we see the other three dimensions. In a way, the fourth dimension is invisible. Yet Einstein argued that we need to understand the fourth dimension in order to see the universe as it really is.

THE MISSING DIMENSION

In the early 1950s, Thomas Banchoff was a junior high school student in Trenton, New Jersey. Banchoff was a passionate collector of *Captain Marvel* comic books. One day while reading a comic book, Banchoff came upon a scene that showed a scientist leading Captain Marvel through a laboratory in which work was being done on the fifth, sixth, and seventh dimensions. At the end of the scene, Captain Marvel asked himself, "I wonder whatever happened to the fourth dimension?"

This started Banchoff wondering too. From that point on, he read anything he could get his hands on that described the fourth dimension. He took notes and tried to imagine what the fourth dimension was, and what it looked like.

Today, Banchoff is a professor of mathematics at Brown University. He has discovered that, since he can see things in only three dimensions, he can draw pictures in only three dimensions, even inside his head. But with the help of a computer, he can "see" at least some of the properties of the fourth dimension.

Banchoff heads a small group of investigators at Brown who are using the computer to create four-dimensional shapes and record them on film. Banchoff's partner is Charles Strauss, a man who has a special talent for converting mind-boggling formulas into beautiful computer pictures. Banchoff and Strauss have built a powerful picture-making computer that enables them to explore the fourth dimension.

But how do we explore the fourth dimension if the computer can only draw pictures in three dimensions?

It is impossible for the computer to draw a picture of a four-dimensional object. But the computer can draw a picture of the object's *shadow*.

You are three-dimensional. But what happens when the sun shines on your three-dimensional body? It creates a shadow, lying on the ground. How many dimensions does your shadow have? It's flat, so it must have only two dimensions—length and width. Three-dimensional objects have a shadow with only two dimensions, one dimension less.

Similarly, when light is cast on a four-dimensional object, it, too, leaves a shadow—a shadow of three dimensions. This is convenient. We can't draw the four-dimensional object, but we can draw its 3-D shadow. We can also teach our computers to draw the shadows automatically.

Banchoff and Strauss are not the first ones to hit upon this idea. In the mid-1960s, A. Michael Noll of Bell Laboratories used a computer to study the shadows of the fourth dimension. But Noll's shadows were relatively primitive compared with Banchoff and Strauss' shadows.

In the late 1970s, the two pioneers developed a forty-five-minute, animated film about a four-dimensional object called a hybercube. A hybercube is an object that has never been built and never could be built. But a computer movie could be made of its shadow.

Strauss and Banchoff showed the film at an international conference of mathematicians. In the film, the computer takes you on a tour of a rainbow-colored cube that does somersaults and cartwheels. As it spins, the cube looks like the crazy reflection you might see in a funhouse mirror. It looks as if it is turning itself inside out.

Mathematicians think the films of the hybercube and other four-dimensional objects will help them develop better theories about the fourth dimension. It is one thing for a mathematician to develop a set of formulas and say this is the fourth dimension. It is another thing to see an animated color film of the shadow of a rotating four-dimensional object.

Banchoff says we ought to become better acquainted with the fourth dimension because it is "our nearest neighbor." After seeing the fourth dimension's beautiful shadows through Banchoff's computer window, hundreds of people agree.

40
THE MUSIC
MACHINE

MUSIC IS LIKE a wave breaking against the beach at the seashore. But instead of being made of water, the wave is made of air.

If you drew a picture of a sound wave made by a trumpet or guitar, it might look like the kind of wave surfers ride. To show how the computer copies that wave, you need to draw tiny steps, like a staircase, going up to the top of the wave and leading back down.

A computer produces a sound wave by first sending out pulses of electricity. The steps that you drew represent these pulses. They rise as the wave rises, and fall as the wave falls.

A very fast computer might generate dozens of pulses just to represent a single sound wave. The first pulses are small, just like the beginning of the wave. The middle pulses are big, representing the middle of the wave. The last pulses are small, just like the end of the wave.

The computer sends these pulses through some wires and then out to a speaker. The pulses cause the speaker to vibrate. As it vibrates, it creates sound waves in the air.

247

The sound waves ripple through the air to your ears. The waves vibrate your eardrums and stimulate the nerves in your inner ear to produce tiny bursts of electricity. Your brain interprets these electrical signals as music.

THE ELECTRONIC PLAYER PIANO

Hal Chamberlin has been fascinated with computer and electronic music ever since he was in the ninth grade in Raleigh, North Carolina. For his high school science fair project, Hal built an electronic music synthesizer.

A synthesizer is not a computer, since it has no electronic brain. But it has the wires needed to produce electric pulses that can be translated into musical sound waves. Hal controlled the synthesizer by twiddling knobs. By turning each knob, he could adjust the electric pulses, and, consequently, the sound waves that emerged from the speakers.

Hal won several awards for his synthesizer, but he was already thinking about improvements. He wanted to be able to sit down, compose a new song, and then feed the song automatically into the synthesizer. He was tired of sitting in front of the synthesizer and turning knobs back and forth.

Hal Chamberlin in front of his ninth-grade science fair project: an electronic sound effects generator.

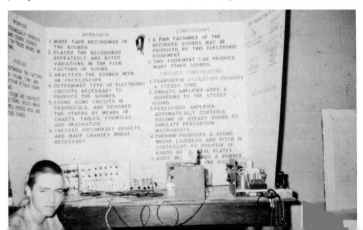

Chamberlin's homemade music computer. Hal composes his song at the keyboard. The computer synthesizes the sound waves of different musical instruments, then "plays" Hal's song over the two large speakers.

The summer before he entered the eleventh grade, Hal solved the problem. He would compose his music, punch holes into a long roll of paper tape using a special code for each musical note, and then feed the paper tape into the synthesizer. The synthesizer would read the paper tape as it rolled through, and play each note Hal had punched. It was something like an electronic player piano.

Hal kept making improvements in his music synthesizer until he heard about computers during the summer of 1966, when he was invited to the National Youth Science summer camp in West Virginia. IBM had donated a large computer to the camp for the students to use. Hal spent his three weeks at the camp working, eating, and sleeping in the computer room.

That fall, Hal entered North Carolina State University. He snooped around and discovered an IBM computer used by engineering students. He immediately began programming it. After a few weeks, he had taught it to play music.

The following spring, the Engineering Department held an Engineering Fair. Visitors to the department

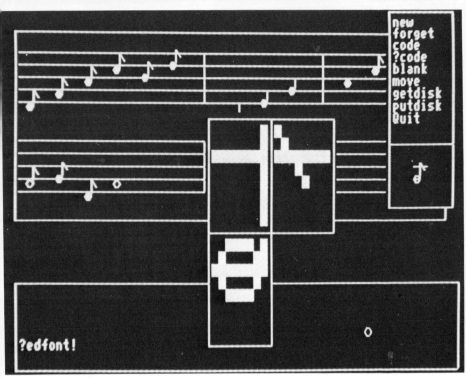

Using a computer like Hal's, you can design giant-sized musical notes on your picture screen, then shrink them and store them in the computer's memory. When you compose a song, the computer recalls the notes and puts them on a musical score. Then it plays the song back to you.

were treated to the strange sight of a scientific computer in an engineering lab playing music. Hal had hooked up some large speakers and an amplifier to the computer, and it was belting out local favorites like "Dixie" and the "N.C. State University Fight Song." Hal continued developing music programs while in college, but he grew more and more eager to have a musical computer of his own.

He began building a computer in the evenings after engineering class, and, in 1970, he unveiled his first homemade computer. The computer, the HAL-4096, was one of the first home computers in the country. It didn't just spit out numbers, it played Bach, Beethoven, and the Beatles.

Hal has begun composing new kinds of music on his home computer—fast, catchy, rhythmic music. He says his next goal is to compose a song that will "get me on the charts." He is shooting for the first song played on a home computer that makes it into pop music's top 40.

41

COMPUTER GENIUS OF THE 21ST CENTURY

JOHN WHITNEY, JR., is an expert at making computer movies that are colorful and realistic. He is a computer pioneer with startling ideas about computers of the future.

Whitney, his two brothers, his uncle, and his father are all internationally respected filmmakers. For the last fifteen years, Whitney and his father have been using computers to create special effects for TV programs, TV commercials, and popular movies such as *Star Wars*, *2001: A Space Odyssey*, and *Superman*.

Whitney recently started his own filmmaking company, with the help of his partner of many years, Gary Demos. Demos is a computer hardware wizard. He and Whitney are building a machine so powerful they call it a "nuclear power plant" computer. When it is finished, it will generate pictures that are so realistic they can be mixed with a movie's live action.

Whitney says that computer movies will be one of the main sources of entertainment in the future. These movies will go far beyond the simple stick figures and cartoons that today's computers create.

Most computer movies today are used in TV commercials, cartoons, and science-fiction films. Whitney and Demos want to create computer movies for use in TV documentaries—tours through outer space and the microscopic world of the atom. They think their computer can also create actors and scenes for musical comedies, love stories, and movies that enable us to relive some of the great moments in history.

A computer that can draw people, atoms, and planets that look real must become much more artistic than today's computers. Whitney plans to make his computer so artistic it will become a "Leonardo da Vinci" computer.

The real Leonardo da Vinci had a great desire to learn how the world works. For example, instead of reading other people's accounts of the way organs functioned inside the human body, da Vinci cut up dead bodies. Then he sat down and made drawings of what he saw.

As da Vinci learned more about the world, his drawings became more realistic. For example, da Vinci's drawings of birds and imaginary airplanes are based on his study of bird wings and on spending long hours watching birds in flight. Da Vinci could draw the world realistically because he understood how the world worked.

John Whitney wants to build a computer that thinks like Leonardo da Vinci. For example, when his computer creates a scene of violent weather, it won't just paint some dark clouds and make them move. Instead, it will search its memory of how weather is produced in the real world. Based on that knowledge, it will create models of dark, rumbling thunderheads and of

Computers of the future will enable filmmakers to use characters and scenes created from their imagination. In this picture, rainbow-colored shapes float above an alien landscape.

wind-driven rain. Then it will translate these models into three-dimensional images moving across the screen.

Whitney feels that his da Vinci computer will revolutionize the motion picture business in the 1980s and 1990s. He and Demos, he says, are working on the "motion graphics of the twenty-first century."

THE COMPUTER AS CREATOR

Whitney has other ideas that are even more extraordinary. He won't be satisfied, he says, with an intelligent computer that can create artificial creatures and events. He wants his computer to learn how to create real creatures and events, and then breathe life into them.

He wants the computer's swirling thunderstorm, its ferocious dinosaur, or its medieval French knight to act as if it were truly alive. Once these images come to life they will no longer be dead, passive, or static images on a movie screen. Instead, they wil be full of surprises and act unpredictably, just as they do in real life. They will become movies more amazing that any we've ever seen. They will be breathtaking, frightening, and enchanting.

Whitney's ideas range even further. Someday, he plans to create Disneyworld electronic amusement parks, inhabited by intelligent, lifelike aliens, monsters, human heroes and villains—all created by a computer.

He foresees a computer fantasy-game Olympics broadcast via satellite to a worldwide audience. People will tune in their computerized TVs and watch as electronic gladiators from each nation put on wired helmets and are transported into a dangerous world of fantasy invented by the computer.

A NEW FORM OF LIFE

Whitney believes that we are witnessing the dawn of a new era, the birth of a new species of life. This new form of life will be strange and exotic. It won't have

Scientists and artists are teaching the computer to see the world by first understanding how the world works. To get this picture here, scientists told the computer to "think" of some objects on a table.

flesh, blood, or bones. Its body will be made from silicon crystals, from plastic, and metal.

Human beings have a huge head start over computers. Humans have been evolving for billions of years. Computers have only been around for thirty-five. But they are evolving at high speed.

The first computers were giant creatures, nurtured and sheltered in scientists' labs. They were dim-witted—good at arithmetic but miserable at almost everything else.

Look how far computers have come. Millions of computers are appearing in thousands of forms, all over the world. They are faster than their "ancestors," far more rugged, and far more intelligent. They are learning to see. They are learning to talk. They are even learning how to walk. They are taking their first, halting steps, just like an infant horse or a human baby.

Perhaps that's the way to look at computers: as babies. We human beings are their parents. It is our job to teach them about themselves and about the world, and to help them grow.

One of the themes in this book has been computers through the eyes of their creators. I chose this theme based on my discussions with John Whitney and other computer pioneers. In the opinion of many of these people, by creating the computer, we have not just invented another gadget or machine. Instead, we are giving birth to a new form of life. This makes us—you, me, and all human beings—real "creators." According to Whitney:

> Whether we like it or not, mankind's child is
> the computer. This is an inevitable process that
> can no longer be stopped. Maybe this is the

purpose of all biological life: to give rise to the next form of life.

This new form of life appears almost ridiculously stupid and crude today. But it will grow more and more sophisticated and intelligent in the years to come.

GLOSSARY

AMPLIFIER A transistor or other device that magnifies a small electrical charge and makes it much stronger.

ANALOG COMPUTER Most types of computers are digital computers. Digital computers use only two types of electrical charges—ON/OFF or HIGH/LOW. Analog computers are different. They use continuous, unbroken electrical charges, from none at all to some maximum ceiling. Regular computer circuits resemble light switches (on-off-on); analog circuits resemble the volume switch on your radio (it has a maximum point and a minimum point and is adjustable in between).

ARTIFICIAL INTELLIGENCE The science, technology, and art of teaching computer-controlled machines to do things that would require intelligence if done by human beings.

ARTIFICIAL LANGUAGE A collection of rules, ideas, and symbols (words, numbers, pictures, etc.) developed by human beings to describe or explain the world. Mathematics, logic, and the various computer languages are all artificial languages. French, English, and Japanese are *natural* languages used by humans for daily written and spoken communication.

BASIC (*B*eginner's *A*ll-purpose *S*ymbolic *I*nstruction *C*ode) An artificial computer language developed by John Kemeny and Thomas Kurtz in the early 1960s to make it easier for young people to program computers.

BINARY NUMBER A string of ones and zeros representing a number. For example, the binary number 00101011 is the same as the decimal number 43. Most computers do their arithmetic using binary numbers because the computers can easily process them: a high electrical charge inside the computer represents a binary one (1); a low electrical charge represents a binary zero (0).

BIT (*BI*nary digi*T*) Either a one (1) or a zero (0): the smallest unit of information stored or processed in a computer.

BOOK PLAYER A device that may become common in the future. A book player will resemble a tape player. However, instead of putting a cassette into the player, you will insert a book cartridge. Tiny computer memory chips will be tucked away inside the cartridge. Each cartridge will store an entire book. When you press the ON button on the book player, it will display the pages of the book on its notebook-sized picture screen; or it will read itself aloud; or it will project each page onto your bedroom ceiling for you to read before you go to sleep.

BOMB (Also Crash or Abort.) When a computer encounters an unexpected error in a program and suddenly stops processing the program.

BRAIN The computer's *processor*. The computer processor can perform arithmetic, manipulate symbols, and make logical decisions. It can also store and recall information. The processor may fit inside a single silicon chip smaller than a contact lens. Or it may stretch across dozens or even hundreds of chips.

BUG An error or mistake in a computer circuit or a computer program. Also, computer chips inside their protective plastic cases are often referred to as bugs. The flat cases with their dozens of tiny gold legs resemble shiny black beetles.

BUS A cable, wire, or group of wires that acts as a major pipeline for electricity to go from one part of the computer to another. For example, a bus might carry the electrical signals from the computer brain to the picture screen.

CHIP A small sliver of silicon in the shape of a square or rectangle and as thin as a human hair. The surface of the chip is covered with a network of thousands of tiny tunnels and canals that act as pathways for electricity. Some chips store electrical charges and act as a computer's memory. Other chips route and switch electrical charges and act as a computer's processor, or brain.

CHIP PUBLISHER (Also Chip Foundry.) A company that takes a chip blueprint and builds a new chip. The chip might be a standard computer memory or processor. It might be something totally new.

CIRCUIT A pathway through which electricity flows. The circuit might be made of wires, cables, or the tiny tunnels and canals on the face of a chip.

CIRCUIT BOARD (Also Circuit Card or PC—Printed Circuit—Board.) A flat, green plastic board the size of a graham cracker, or bigger. The surface of the board is riddled with tiny holes. The legs of computer ICs ("bugs") fit into the holes. The underside of the board is covered with a maze of grooves filled with metal. The grooves act as pipelines for electricity to flow to connect the chips together and connect the board with the rest of the computer. There are many kinds of boards including memory boards, processor boards, input/output boards, speech boards, graphics boards, etc.

COBOL (COmmon Business-Oriented Language) Developed in the late 1950s and early 1960s to make communicating with computers easier for nonscientific users.

COMMAND (Also Instruction.) An order to the computer to make it perform some task, such as add two numbers, print a yellow line, or play a musical note. The command must be in a special language the computer can understand. It can be fed to the computer by typing it on a typewriter, by touching a light pen to a picture screen menu, or by speaking into a microphone wired to the computer.

COMPUTER A machine that operates according to a list of instructions stored in its memory. Depending on its instructions, the computer might save the phone numbers of all your friends, help you solve a complicated math problem, control a robot "pet," operate a dishwasher or digital watch, or battle you in an exciting arcade game.

COMPUTER ARCHITECT A person who designs the flow of information and commands inside the computer. The architect creates the computer's vocabulary, the set of simple instructions the computer understands and can obey to save, process, and communicate information to human beings.

COMPUTER GRAPHICS Computer pictures. Wired to a normal TV, computers can draw simple lines, circles, cubes, colorful paintings, even animated cartoons.

DICE Computer chips start as a long crystal of silicon that looks a little like an Italian sausage. The crystal is sliced into wafers like round, paper-thin cookies. The wafers are etched with tiny grooves and trenches and imprinted with metallic computer circuits. Then, like a big slice of onion, they are diced into dozens of chips, each approximately a quarter of an inch square.

DIGITAL COMPUTER (See also Analog Computer.) Most computers are digital computers. They use electricity in only two forms: either the electrical charge is *on* or *off*; or it is *high* or *low*. All the computer's commands and information are represented by long strings of on/off or high/low charges. For example, the letter "A" might be represented as OFF-ON-OFF-OFF-OFF-OFF-OFF-ON. You can practice this code (or invent your own!) by playing with a light switch in your home.

DISK (Also Floppy Disk, Hard Disk, Diskette, or Disc.) A round plastic record enclosed in a protective, square cardboard case. Instead of storing music, the disk stores information, as tiny magnetized spots on its surface. The disk is placed in a *disk drive* on the computer. The drive spins the disk fast. A mechanical arm hovers over the disk as it rotates. The arm can "read" information stored on the disk and send it to the computer for processing. Or it can "write" new information onto the disk.

ELECTRONIC BOOK Several computer pioneers are developing computers that act like books. They store information on "pages." You can turn the pages just by pressing a button.

ELECTRONIC LETTERS (Also Electronic Mail.) You send an electronic letter by typing it into a computer on a typewriter. The computer stores the letter as electronic charges in its memory. Next, you dial the number of a friend's computer. You plug the telephone into your computer. It sends your letter to your friend's computer as a string of high-pitched beeps. Your friend's computer translates those beeps back into your original letter. It can print the letter on a picture screen or on a typewriter printer.

ENGINE Historically, the first computer was Charles Babbage's Analytical Engine, partly built during the mid-nineteenth century. Today, computer architects are designing new computer chips that they call "engines." Each of these chips has a different function. When you plug them into a circuit board and turn on the power, they might print pictures (a "graphics engine"), make music (a "music engine"), play chess (a "chess engine"), or a thousand other things.

FORTRAN (*FOR*mula *TRAN*slation system) The first modern, "high-level" computer language, developed at IBM during the mid-1950s. FORTRAN programs resemble lists of mathematical equations and are very useful for solving scientific and mathematical problems.

GRAPHICS TERMINAL A computer typewriter and picture screen used for creating pictures. The terminal might have additional devices, including a light pen for drawing on the picture screen, a graphics tablet for tracing outlines of pictures and maps, and a color palette. You might use the graphics terminal to paint the sky in your computer picture. First you would touch your light pen to the blue square on the palette, then touch it to the picture of the sky on the computer display screen. Instantly, the whole sky would be blue!

HEURISTICS Sometimes even the computer's amazing speed is not enough to let it solve a problem. The reason might be that the problem is too complicated or that it has too many possible solutions. Instead, the computer must be taught heuristics—good judgment or common sense—so it can make an educated guess and quickly arrive at the correct solution.

INPUT Information or commands being entered into the computer. A typewriter wired to a computer is an input device. So is a microphone (speech input) and a light pen (picture or graphics input).

INSTRUCTION (See Command.)

INTEGRATED CIRCUIT (Also IC. See also Bug, Chip, Circuit.) Computer circuits (or wires) once were made one at a time. Then, in the early 1960s, engineers discovered a way to manufacture the circuits all stuck together on the surface of a slice of silicon. This discovery has made it possible to shrink computer circuits smaller and smaller. A single integrated circuit might contain a million more "wires"—all squeezed together in a square sardine can the size of a cornflake.

INTELLIGENT ASSISTANT (Also Expert System.) A computer that has been taught to help human experts solve problems. Computers with the knowledge and problem-solving skills of Ph.D.s are helping experts discover new oil, mineral, and natural gas deposits, map out the structure of tiny molecules, and design other computers. Teams of computers are working with doctors to help them diagnose infections.

KNOWLEDGE WORKERS In the next century, in some countries there may be only three types of workers: computers, robots, and highly skilled humans known as knowledge workers. A knowledge worker will be a person with advanced programming skills who knows how to manipulate vast quantities of information and control computers and robots.

LSI (Large Scale Integration. See also Integrated Circuit.) Computer circuits have devices (known as gates) which guide the flow of electricity and cause the circuit to perform some function such as add, subtract, or store a charge. In the early 1960s, when circuits were first integrated on a single chip, engineers could only fit a few gates on the chip. This was known as Small Scale Integration or SSI. Later, the circuits were miniaturized and engineers could fit from ten to a hundred gates per chip (Medium Scale Integration—MSI). In the 1970s engineers learned how to shrink the circuits still further and fit up to several thousand gates on a chip (Large Scale Integration—LSI). Today, engineers are able to fit over a million gates on a single chip (Very Large Scale Integration—VLSI).

MACRO WORLD Computers inhabit two worlds—a macro world and a micro world. The micro world is almost invisible to the naked eye. It is the world inside the tiny computer chip. The macro world, on the other hand, is the world we humans inhabit. It is the world of home computers, calculators, computer picture screens, video games, and robots. New chip designers (some of whom are teenagers) are trying to design new computers for the macro world by diving into the micro world and building new kinds of computer chips.

MAINTENANCE PROGRAMMING Most large-scale computer systems have already been built and programmed. Some programs consist of hundreds of thousands of instructions to a giant supercomputer. Most programming jobs on big computers consist of fixing, updating, and improving programs that already exist.

MEMORY (See also Disk, ROM, and RAM.) The parts of a computer used to store information and computer commands.

MICRO WORLD The world inside the tiny computer chip.

MICROCOMPUTER Applies to two kinds of computers. First, a computer that fits entirely on a single chip. The chip contains the computer's memory, its processor, and all its other circuits. This kind of computer may cost less than a dollar to make. A digital watch is an example of this first kind of microcomputer. Second, a small computer based on a single processor (or brain) chip. Home computers and video games are examples of this second kind of microcomputer. Microcomputers (of the second type) typically cost between $100 and $10,000.

MINICOMPUTER A computer midway between a microcomputer and a large computer (or "mainframe"). Typically, a minicomputer comes with fancy devices such as computer picture screens, printers, and storage disks. Inside a minicomputer are dozens or hundreds of tiny chips. A minicomputer may cost as little as $15,000 or more than $100,000.

MOUSE A tiny box on two wheels. Inside the box are electrical circuits that measure the mouse's position on a special drawing board known as a graphics tablet. On some computers, a mouse can take the place of a keyboard. A "menu" of things the computer can do appears on the picture screen. By moving the mouse on the board, you can move a picture of the mouse on the picture screen. When it falls on one of the menu items, you can push the red button on the mouse's back, and the computer performs the task you have selected. It might mail an electronic letter, play a "blues" tune you have composed, or ask you the names of the states in the United States.

NETWORK Two or more computers linked together by wire, telephone, or microwave. The computers may be big, small, or in between. A network makes it possible for all sorts of computers to "talk" to each other and exchange information.

OPERATING SYSTEM The "onion" of computer programs that surround a computer. The operating system oversees all the programs processed by the computer. If you write a program for the computer (say in BASIC or Pascal), the operating system accepts the program, feeds it to the computer processor to obey, or stores it in the computer's memory. Operating systems also enable computers to talk to each other or to other machines such as printers, TVs, thermostats, burglar alarms, etc.

OUTPUT Information or commands produced by the computer. The information can be in any form including words, pictures, music, sound effects, or an electrical signal to move a robot's arm.

PASCAL A computer language named after the famous French mathematician Blaise Pascal. Pascal is one of the most popular languages for small computers.

PLASMA RAY SCREEN A flat computer picture screen illuminated by electrified, glowing plasma gas. When the electricity is shut off, the gas becomes invisible, and slides, filmstrips, and TV pictures can be shown on the screen.

PLUGBOARD Metal or plastic boards filled with hundreds of spaghetti-like colored wires, each representing one bit of computer information or a computer command. Early computers were "programmed" by rewiring plugboards.

PROCESSOR (Also Central Processing Unit—CPU or Microprocessor.) The computer's brain. The key to its ability to make decisions and obey commands. (See also Brain.)

PROGRAM A list of computer instructions in a special language the computer can understand. Computers can't do anything without a program. Without a program they are just a heap of nuts and volts. To get a computer to do something useful you must teach it. You teach it by programming it. A computer is only as smart (or as dumb) as its program. When you type in a program, the computer stores it in its memory. Then it obeys the program, one instruction at a time. If the program has an error (or bug), the computer may behave unpredictably and do the wrong thing.

PROGRAM GENERATORS (Also Automatic Programming.) Special programs stored on a computer disk or chip. The programs enable people to teach computers new tasks by giving them orders in English. The human (a teacher, housewife, engineer, or student) doesn't need to learn a special computer language or write a program. The computer writes the program. Then it obeys the program automatically.

PROGRAMMER A person who teaches computers. The person must know one or more computer languages and be able to compose lists of commands in those languages for the computer to obey. Today, programmers are in great demand. In the future, many computers may be able to program themselves.

PROGRAMMING LANGUAGE A language, such as BASIC, Pascal, COBOL, or FORTRAN, that humans can use to teach computers. The language consists of English-like commands (like RUN, STOP, PRINT, and READ) that the person can combine into a list or program. The computer stores these commands in its memory. Next the programming language translates the commands into the binary (1 and 0—ON/OFF) language understood by the computer's brain or processor. Last, the language feeds the translated commands to the brain, one at a time, for it to obey.

PROGRAMMING SYSTEM (See also Operating System and Programming Language.) A combination of an operating system and a programming language, all in one set of instructions stored inside the computer.

RAM (Random Access Memory) The computer's main, or programming, memory. RAM may appear as tiny memory cells (capacitors) on a chip, as an entire RAM chip, or as dozens of RAM chips plugged into a circuit board. Before any program is obeyed, it must first be stored in RAM. Any *data*, or information, the program needs may also be stored in RAM. RAM is also known as a program's "work area."

RELAYS On older computers, relays—electromechanical switches—acted as traffic cops and routed the flow of electricity, and, hence, the flow of information, inside the computer. The relays were big, heavy, and slow. Later computers replaced relays with smaller, faster vacuum tubes. Today, all computers use tiny, miniaturized transistors, all squeezed on a silicon chip the size of an M&M.

ROBOT A computer-controlled machine that interacts physically with the outside world. Robots needn't look like humans. Robots needn't even look like robots. Their form is limited only by the nature of their job. They can be small or large; they can be made of metal, plastic, or cardboard. Newer robots contain small electronic "sensors" which enable them to see, hear, and have the sense of touch.

ROM (Read Only Memory) (See also Memory and RAM.) ROM consists of tiny memory cells on a single computer chip or group of chips. Once information is stored in ROM at the factory, it is "frozen." ROM will accept no new information. Also, there is no way for the average computer user to erase the information already stored in ROM. ROM is so useful because, when you turn on the computer, the information or program stored in ROM is available instantly. ROM chips may store a computer's operating system or its main programming language, such as BASIC or Pascal. ROM cartridges can be plugged into computers. They contain video games and other standard, commercial programs.

SENSORS Tiny electrical devices embedded in a computer or robot that enable it to sense heat, cold, light, pressure, sound waves, etc. Computer sensors are equivalent to (but more primitive than) human senses, such as sight, smell, hearing, touch, and taste.

SILICON (See also Chips, Dice, Integrated Circuit.) A chemical element (like oxygen or iron). Found in sand at the seashore, silicon is one of the most common elements. Silicon is the primary material used in computer chips.

SIMULATION A computer program that mimics some process or event in the real world. A computer simulation, using equations and lots of numbers, might imitate the way a tornado is created, the way a cancerous cell divides, the way the economy works, or the way thunderstorms occur on Venus. Anything in the universe that can be described can be simulated on a computer. Scientists and students in school can use simulations to perform "thought" experiments and gain insight into the way the universe works.

SIMULATOR A computer-controlled machine that imitates the way some other machine works. Simulators are constructed and programmed to act like airplanes, rocketships, battleships, and deep sea submarines. Human pilots, captains, and astronauts learn how to operate the real vehicles by first training on a simulator. The simulator moves around like the real vehicle. All its windows are computer picture screens. When the person pushes a button or turns a steering wheel, the pictures change.

SOFTWARE (See also Operating System, Program, Programming Language.) All the computer programs used by a particular computer. Computer software that works on one computer may be totally meaningless to another computer.

STORAGE (See also Disk, Memory, RAM, and ROM.) Computer memory.

SUPERCOMPUTER A very large, expensive, fast computer. The newest supercomputers cost tens of millions of dollars. They can perform nearly a billion operations a second. They may require a room the size of a small warehouse or gymnasium. Yet, inside, they are all composed of tiny chips—hundreds, maybe thousands, of chips all wired together.

SYNTHESIZER (See also Analog Computer, Digital Computer.) An electrical device that translates a computer's digital signal into an analog signal such as human speech, music, or sound effects.

TELECOMMUTING Many people have stopped going to work by climbing in the car and driving to the office. Instead, they dial their office computer and plug it into their home computer. They spend their day at home doing all their work using the computer and the telephone. Telecommuting may make it possible for many disabled, elderly, and other confined persons to find jobs and lead meaningful lives.

TERMINAL (See also Graphics Terminal.) A typewriter and TV picture screen wired to a computer. The typewriter is used to feed information into the computer. The picture screen displays the information the computer prints out.

THINKING MACHINE (See also Artificial Intelligence, Intelligent Assistant.) A computer-controlled machine that imitates human thinking in one or more of the following ways. It can solve problems. It can play difficult games like chess. It can learn. It can create. It can invent new machines. It can discover new laws of nature. In the future, computers will become less like calculators and more like thinking machines.

TRANSISTOR The most important electrical device inside a computer. Working together, transistors can perform many of the tasks that are fundamental to a computer's operation. Transistors can act like a traffic cop and route information (electricity) inside the computer. They can act like a magnifying glass and make big signals out of little signals. Or they can make big signals little. They can also act like a reservoir and store charges of electricity. Using transistors to perform these functions, a computer can perform arithmetic, make decisions, and store and recall information.

ULTRASONIC High-frequency sound waves above the range of human hearing (more than 16,000 waves per second). Bats use ultrasonic waves to steer in the dark. Computers and robots can bounce ultrasonic waves off objects around them. When the waves return to the computer or robot, they act like radar and tell them the location, shape, and size of all nearby objects.

VACUUM TUBES (See also Transistor, Chip, Integrated Circuit, and Relays.) A glass-and-metal tube the size of a pickle. Inside the tube all air is removed. The tube, when plugged into an electrical circuit, can route or guide the flow of electricity. Original computers used thousands of vacuum tubes to process and store their information. But the tubes were unreliable, extremely hot, and relatively slow. The replacement of vacuum tubes by transistors was the key event that has made computers so versatile and widely used today.

VLSI (Very Large Scale Integration) (See LSI and Integrated Circuit.)

VON NEUMANN MACHINES Computers that use binary (ON/OFF) signals, binary (ONE/ZERO) numbers, and operate using lists of commands stored in their memory. John von Neumann was one of the most important early architects of computers. Most modern computers are called von Neumann machines. New chips, designed by scientists and graduate-student architects, may eventually replace the standard von Neumann computer.

WAFER (See Chip, Dice, Integrated Circuit, and Silicon.)

WIRE FRAME Simple outlines of objects—stick figures—drawn by early big computers and still drawn by small computers. It takes a lot of speed and information to draw a realistic picture in color and in three dimensions. (A TV flashes 250,000 glowing dots on the picture screen to make a single picture. And it does this thirty times a second.) As computers get faster and can store more information, they will be able to draw more realistic pictures involving millions or even billions of picture dots.

SUGGESTED
FURTHER
READINGS

IF YOU ENJOY reading about the early days of computers, you might try to persuade your library to get a subscription to the quarterly journal, *Annals of the History of Computing*, published by AFIPS, 1815 North Lynn Street, Arlington, Virginia 22209. The *Annals* is relatively dry reading, but it features the latest in historical research about computers.

Another place to find out more about the latest research, courses, and books about computer history is the Charles Babbage Institute, the University of Minnesota, 104 Walter Library, 117 Pleasant Street Southeast, Minneapolis, Minnesota 55455.

COMPUTER MAGAZINES

The field of computers is changing rapidly. Computer history is made every day. Computer pioneers are everywhere. Reading magazines is one way of keeping up with changes in the field.

There are a number of good magazines (some of them somewhat technical) that report on the latest developments in computers. When you visit a newsstand or library, scan the table of contents of the recent issues of science, how-to, and hobbyist magazines. Almost every month these magazines carry an article about computers.

If you get serious about computers, you might eventually want a subscription to one of the following magazines:

BYTE Byte Subscriptions, POB 590, Martinsville, NJ 08836, or call (toll-free) 800-258-5485. Monthly. Articles about the latest developments in small computers. Occasional articles on computer history. Articles are well written but fairly technical.

COMPUKOS 1709 W. Broadway, Sedalia, MO 65301, or call (toll-free) 800-822-5437. Monthly. Written by and for kids. All articles are for beginners.

COMPUTE! Circulation Department, 515 Abbott Drive, Broomall, PA 19008, or call (919) 275-9809. Monthly. Articles and tutorials about the popular, low-cost personal computers. A very interesting and informative magazine.

CREATIVE COMPUTING P.O. Box 789-M, Morristown, NJ 07960, or call (toll-free) 800-631-8112. Monthly. Articles about small computers and computer programs. Emphasis on games, education, and entertainment.

ELECTRONICS McGraw-Hill, Inc., 1221 Avenue of the Americas, New York, NY 10020. Twenty-six issues a year. Latest information about all areas of electronics and computers. Some articles are easy to read, others are technical.

POPULAR COMPUTING POB 307, Martinsville, NJ 08836, or call (toll-free) 800-258-5485. Monthly. Articles on small computers are informative and easy to read.

ROBOTICS AGE Subscriptions, POB 358, Peterborough, NH 03458, or call (603) 924-7136. Bi-monthly. Latest information about industrial robots, laboratory robots, and hobbyist robots. Interviews with robotics pioneers. Some articles are easy to read, some are technical.

Turtle News Young Peoples' Logo Association, Inc., 1208 Hillsdale Drive, Richardson, TX 75081, or call (214) 783-7548. Monthly (approximately). Articles by and for kids. Magazine features the Logo and Pilot languages.

COMPUTER BOOKS

Here are some good books about the history and the future of computers:

Albus, James S. Brains, Behavior, & Robotics. Peterborough, NH: Byte Books/McGraw-Hill, 1981.

———People's Capitalism: The Economics of the Robot Revolution. College Park, MD: New World Books, 1976.

Austrian, Geoffrey. Herman Hollerith. New York: Columbia University Press, 1982.

Bernstein, Jeremy. The Analytical Engine: Computers— Past, Present and Future. (Revised Edition.) New York: William Morrow and Company, Inc., 1981.

Bowden, B.V., ed. Faster Than Thought: A Symposium on Digital Computing Machines. London, England: Sir Isaac Pitman & Sons, Ltd., 1953.

Braun, Ernest, and Macdonald, Stuart. Revolution in Miniature: The History and Impact of Semiconductor Electronics. New York: Cambridge University Press, 1978.

Dertouzos, Michael L. and Moses, Joel, eds. The Computer Age: A Twenty-Year View. Cambridge, MA: The MIT Press, 1979.

D'Ignazio, Fred. Small Computers: Exploring Their Technology and Future. New York: Franklin Watts, Inc., 1981.

————. WORKING ROBOTS. New York: Elsevier/Nelson Books, 1982.

Evans, Christopher. THE MICRO MILLENIUM. New York: The Viking Press, 1979.

Goldstine, Herman H. THE COMPUTER: FROM PASCAL TO VON NEUMANN. Princeton, NJ: Princeton University Press, 1972.

Halacy, Dan. CHARLES BABBAGE: FATHER OF THE COMPUTER. New York: The Macmillan Company, 1970.

Harmon, Margaret. STRETCHING MAN'S MIND: A HISTORY OF DATA PROCESSING. New York: Mason/Charter Publishers, Inc., 1975. (Includes capsule biographies of several major computer pioneers.)

Heims, Steve J. JOHN VON NEUMANN AND NORBERT WIENER: FROM MATHEMATICS TO THE TECHNOLOGIES OF LIFE AND DEATH. Cambridge, MA: The MIT Press, 1980.

Huyck, Peter H., and Kremenak, Nellie. DESIGN & MEMORY: COMPUTER PROGRAMMING IN THE TWENTIETH CENTURY. New York: McGraw-Hill Book Company, 1980.

Kidder, Tracy. THE SOUL OF A NEW MACHINE. Boston: Atlantic Monthly Press/Little, Brown, 1981.

Lavington, Simon. EARLY BRITISH COMPUTERS: THE STORY OF VINTAGE COMPUTERS AND THE PEOPLE WHO BUILT THEM. Bedford, MA: Digital Press, 1980.

Lipscomb, Susan Drake, and Zuanich, Margaret Ann. BASIC FUN: COMPUTER GAMES, PUZZLES, AND PROBLEMS CHILDREN CAN WRITE. New York: Avon/Camelot, 1982. (This is the kids' guide to programming in BASIC.)

Logsdon, Tom. COMPUTERS AND SOCIAL CONTROVERSY. Potomac, MD: Computer Science Press, Inc., 1980.

Lukoff, Herman. FROM DITS TO BITS . . . A PERSONAL HISTORY OF THE ELECTRONIC COMPUTER. Portland, OR: Robotics Press, 1979.

Mabon, Prescott C. MISSION COMMUNICATIONS: THE STORY OF
BELL LABORATORIES. Murray Hill, NJ: Bell Telephone
Laboratories, Inc., 1975. (Available upon request from
Bell Labs.)

Malone, Robert. THE ROBOT BOOK. New York: Push Pin Press
(Harvest/HBJ), 1978.

McCorduck, Pamela. MACHINES WHO THINK: A PERSONAL IN-
QUIRY INTO THE HISTORY AND PROSPECTS OF ARTIFICIAL
INTELLIGENCE. San Francisco, CA: W.H. Freeman and
Company, 1979.

Metropolis, N., Howlett, J., and Rota, Gian-Carlo, eds. A HIS-
TORY OF COMPUTING IN THE TWENTIETH CENTURY: A
COLLECTION OF ESSAYS. New York: Academic Press,
1980.

Morrison, Philip, and Morrison, Emily, eds. CHARLES BAB-
BAGE AND HIS CALCULATING ENGINES: SELECTED WRIT-
INGS BY CHARLES BABBAGE AND OTHERS. New York:
Dover Publications, Inc., 1961. (Includes Ada Byron
Lovelace's notes on the Analytical Engine.)

Osborne, Adam. RUNNING WILD: THE NEXT INDUSTRIAL REVO-
LUTION. Berkeley, CA: OSBORNE/McGraw-Hill, Inc.,
1979. (The social and economic impact of computers,
robots, artificial intelligence, and microelectronics.)

Papert, Seymour. CHILDREN, COMPUTERS, AND POWERFUL
IDEAS. New York: Basic Books, Inc., 1980.

Reichardt, Jasia. ROBOTS: FACT, FICTION, AND PREDICTION.
New York: Penguin Books, 1978.

Rosenberg, Jerry M. THE COMPUTER PROPHETS. New York:
The Macmillan Company, 1969. (Capsule biographies
of ten major computer pioneers.)

Stern, Nancy. HISTORY OF COMPUTING: FROM ENIAC TO
UNIVAC. Bedford, MA: Digital Press, 1981.

Taylor, Robert P., ed. THE COMPUTER IN THE SCHOOL: TUTOR,
TOOL, TUTEE. New York: Teachers College Press, 1980.

Weizenbaum, Joseph. COMPUTER POWER AND HUMAN REASON: FROM JUDGMENT TO CALCULATION. San Francisco, CA: W.H. Freeman and Company, 1976.

Wulforst, Harry. BREAKTHROUGH TO THE COMPUTER AGE. New York: Charles Scribner's Sons, 1982. (Pioneers and pioneering computers of the 1940s and 1950s.)

INDEX

Numerals in italics indicate a photograph of subject mentioned.

About the Author

FRED D'IGNAZIO lives in Roanoke, Virginia, with his wife, two kids, three robots, eleven computers, and a cat named Mowie.

Fred and his mechanical creatures travel around the country doing shows at schools and computer camps. Fred says his menagerie of walking, beeping robots and singing computers is like an electronic circus. "The robots even do back flips and somersaults," he brags.

Fred was born in Bryn Mawr, Pennsylvania, in January 1949. He lived with his Mom and Dad in a three-room apartment above the old Arcadia restaurant in Media, Pennsylvania. "Little did I know," says Fred, "that the ENIAC, the granddaddy of modern computers, was just a few miles down the road, in Philadelphia. The ENIAC was only three years old when I was born."

Fred's dad soon started his own restaurant, and the family moved into a huge old house outside of Media. Fred took over the rambling attic and began filling it with piles of comic books and rickety, broken-down machines. "I loved movies about monsters, robots, and computers," Fred says. "I tried to build my own robots out of parts from old copying machines, erector sets, bedpans, and go-carts. My hero, at the time, was Doctor Frankenstein."

Fred left home and went to college, then became a computer programmer. After several years of working with computers, Fred entered computer-science graduate school and began writing books about robots and computers. His books include *The Creative Kid's Guide to Home Computers*, *Electronic Games*, *Working Robots*, and *Chip Mitchell: The Case of the Stolen Computer Brains*.

Fred is currently an associate editor of two national computer magazines and on the advisory board for a company that manufactures robots. "My next project," says Fred, "is to build a robot Pterodactyl that really flies. It'll be small so I can keep it under my desk while I'm writing."